C000242795

Wolverhampton Memories

The publishers would like to thank the following companies for their support in the production of this book

Armitage Shanks

Burns & Dudgon Limited

Compton Hospice

Fern Plastic Products

Freshway Foods

H Goodall Limited

JT Jarvis & Son Limited

George Kertland & Son

Newbridge Preparatory School

Millers Jewellers

Pepito

The Wulfrun Centre

First published in Great Britain by True North Books Limited
England HX5 9AE
01422 377977

ISBN 1 903204 50 X

Text, design and origination by True North Books Limited
Printed and bound by The Amadeus Press Limited

Wolverhampton Memories

Contents

Introduction

Turn the pages with care reader, and enjoy the memories evoked by the photographs contained within this book. Let each be a spark to light fond memories of an ever changing town. With hindsight, judge the wisdom of the alterations made in the name of progress; but be gentle, for those who made the changes did so for what they thought to be the very best of reasons at the time. If necessary, mourn the passing and the loss of landmarks that were a part of your own personal historys. Be wary, though, lest the rose-coloured spectacles that we always wear when we revisit our childhood influence your judgements.

It is thought that Wolverhampton gets its name from a derivation of the Saxon name for the area, 'Heantun', which means 'high town', and the Lady Wulfruna who granted the lands to a monastery. 'Wulfruna's Heantun', through usage changed, and in the charter of King William I in 1078 AD there was a reference to 'Wlurehamton'; developing through the centuries to the name of Wolverhampton.

Originally the wealth of Wolverhampton, and the surrounding country, had been based, as in many other parts of the land, on wool. With the discovery of coal and ironstone in the ground, those early origins were soon lost in the smoke and grime that bellowed from the furnaces and the pits. The industrial era also brought many social injustices. Investigations into cheap child labour would have elicited the response, 'You say they shouldn't be working 'til they're ten years old? They're in the pits long before that age! Ah, and the wives too!' A wife would have taken food to her husband working in the mine and continued filling the carts whilst he ate. They would come out carrying the heavy basket of coal, which was their free entitlement. At least they would not be cold even if they were hungry.

The locksmiths learned their skills and applied their art, whilst the ironmasters or 'chapmen', often had interests in a number of business ventures. The Molineux family were a typical example. Thomas Molineux owned a house at the bottom of Dudley Street, approximately where Marks and

Queen's Square in the 1950s.

Spencer's now stands. His brother, Benjamin, built a house on the site where the Molineux Hotel was later erected. The football club held its inaugural meetings here and the land, where the ground was built, was owned by this family. The stand still bears their name.

To the modern visitor, the 'Black Country' must seem a strange name to give to this green and pleasant area, and certainly to the warmth and hospitality to be found in the bright and friendly city of Wolverhampton. The name is now only a reminder of the past history, which forged, not only the metal, but also the very character of the people who turned that metal into works of engineering art. The car industry of the Midlands developed where the raw materials were to be found, and companies, like Goodyear and others, brought prosperity and fame.

The Wulfrunians were early victims of the recession. A small taste of how difficult life must have been for the working people is reflected in a newspaper article in the Express and Star newspaper dated 28th January 1937. Bearing the title, 'Signs of prosperity at the pawnbrokers', the report said that

A bustling Dudley Street in 1946.

'there are many signs of recovery from the recession 'there are fewer pledges and more articles are being redeemed than there have been for a considerable time'. 'Wives', the article went on to report, 'are wearing their wedding rings again'! It would seem that the people had more to occupy their time than to worry too much about the civil war, which was raging in Spain, or the alleged involvement and interference from Germany's Mr Hitler or his Italian allies.

But history has a way of turning full circle, and even the trams have returned. Wulfrunians smile knowingly and tell strangers that the new Metro trams were necessary in order to give the people of Birmingham a chance to enjoy the culture and refinement of Wolverhampton. With determination the people of the city have cast another image from the iron. Proud to have acquired city status, Wolverhampton justifiably boasts of an excellent University, of new industries, of its magnificent shopping centres, and the recently expanded science park. Whoever first composed the city's motto, could not have known how appropriate it would turn out to be. 'Out of darkness cometh light'.

Around the city centre

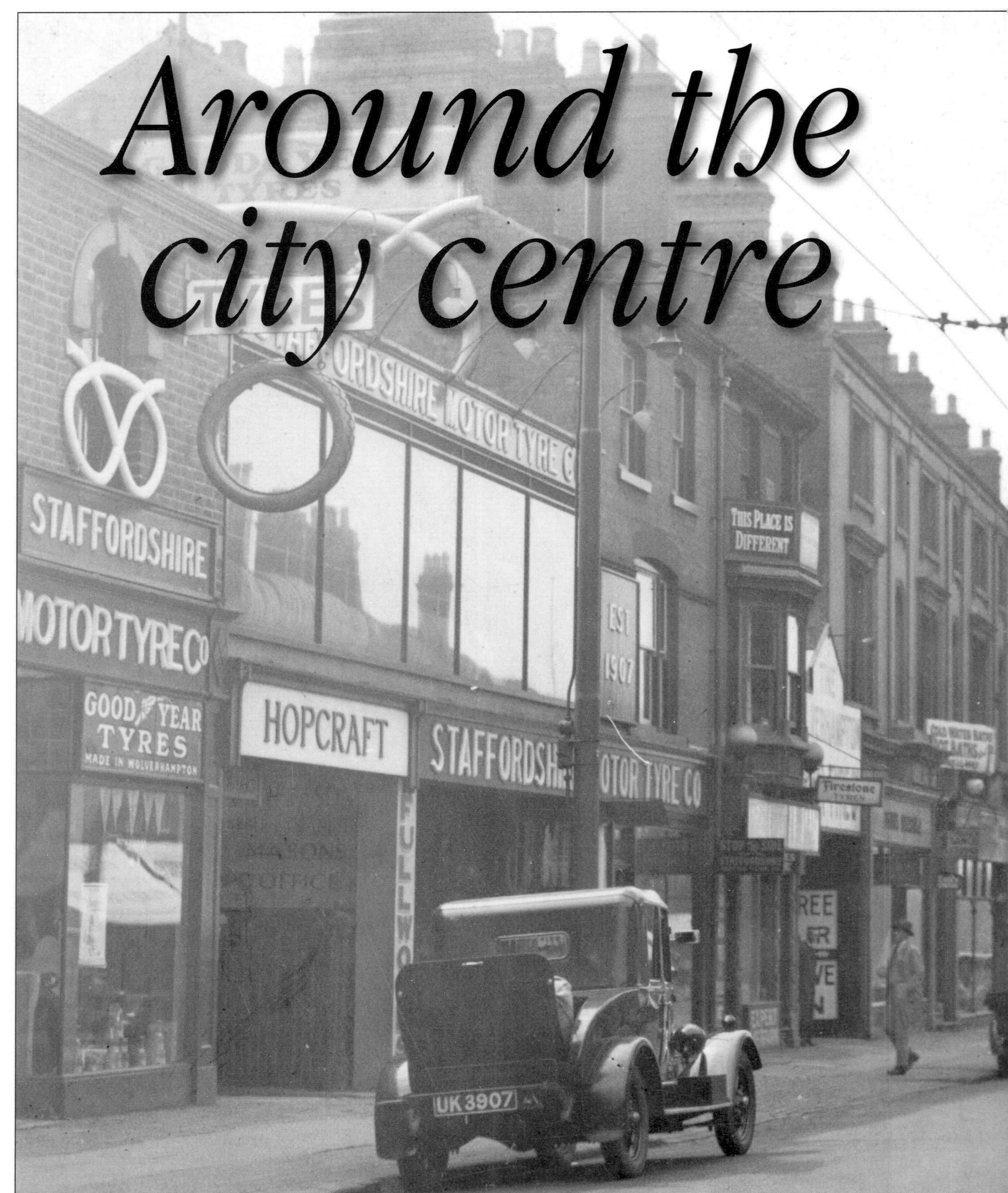

On a pleasant and sunny day in the late twenties, or early thirties, it was certainly warm enough for the Austin to roll back its' canvas roof, for the shops to need to pull down the blinds to protect their window displays, and for the car in the foreground to leave the 'dickey-seat' open to the elements. It is a wonder that this spare seat in the boot has not been reintroduced in modern car design. How useful it would be when carrying passengers with whom the driver finds difficulty in holding a meaningful conversation. A simple step on the rear mudguard and they could be seated quietly in the open air until journey's end had been reached. Such a design seems useful for carrying new Goodyear tyres from the Staffordshire Motor Tyre Company's store in Chapel Ash. There is plenty of time to load. No parking problems here. No traffic warden. Not a single yellow line in sight. Trolley buses are now in service, introduced in 1927. The Guy Motor Company built them.
Along the road can be seen a three-wheeler bike, with, what appears to be a carrying box. Can this be a 'stop-me-and-buy-one' vendor? Choc Ice-creams were introduced in 1927 and ice cream was expensive, but popular. Or perhaps he is selling the Mars Bar, which, according to the adverts, gave enough energy to help us to 'work, rest and play'. It had been introduced a decade earlier in 1920. Its partner, which you could 'eat between meals without ruining your appetite', the Milky Way, had been in existence since 1923. They have not aged at all, have they?

Below: A misty morning scene in Queen's Square c1950, a mist, which often lifts as the winter sun gently warms it. In the fifties though, that toxic killer, smog, could be produced. Under certain weather conditions, a lethal cocktail of smoke, from domestic as well as factory chimneys, and fog, combined. They produced a cloud that could roll up the road like something from an early science fiction film. Maybe they were the inspiration for the Quatermass science fiction stories. The air could be clear ahead of the cloud, but once enveloped by it, it was so thick that the headlights of a car made little difference. In some circumstances the light was reflected back and visibility was worse. The dilemma was that others had to see you. The old Ford popular had a mechanically powered windscreen wiper, which slowed almost to a stop when the engine was labouring, but swung too and fro frantically the moment the foot was lifted from the accelerator. Perhaps it isn't a fog after all, but just the smoke from one of Churchill's cigars. He became Prime Minister again in 1951 at the ripe old age of seventy-seven. Pedestrians seem not to have understood the purpose of the studs in the road that mark a crossing. Only the trolley bus has 'lines' to restrict its route. The rest drive where they wish. Forget the weather and rush home to listen to that new show on the radio 'The Goon Show', or that story about the lives of simple country folk. What is it called? Oh, yes! 'The Archers'. Isn't it hard now not to sing the theme tune whenever the programme is mentioned?

Right: Just look at the length of that car bonnet as it moves down Dudley Street. In a modern car the bonnet dips away out of sight, but on such a vehicle it stretched forever, until the driver felt that he wasn't driving this monster, but simply aiming it. Built on a chassis such cars were like the earlier coaches. A heavy engine had simply replaced the horse. Even the rear windows owed more to the stagecoach for their design than to the practical consideration of being able to see what was following, or rear visibility when reversing. More important by far was the elegance and style. They smelt of leather and moved with all the easy grace of a well-furnished drawing room. Overhead is a complex web of power lines for the trolley buses. A junction, like the one above the Prince Consort's head, invariably caused the pantographs to become disengaged from the lines if the driver over-estimated the speed. With a flash and shower of tiny sparks on a cold day, the arm would spring above. Usually accompanied by cheers from any school children, who might be travelling on the top deck. Do you remember the conductors who made you sit downstairs if you were not quick to run up before they could say anything? Traffic came to a standstill whilst the conductor pulled the long bamboo pole, with the hook attached, from its place in a tube beneath the bus. Once he had caught the ring on the arm he would swing it back into place. As the arm came near the wire it would be grabbed by a magnetic force and held in place.

Above right: Careless talk costs lives we were told during the second world war. But money didn't talk carelessly, as can be seen from this wartime photograph of Queen's Square. The sign on the plinth of Prince Albert's equestrian statue reads 'Money Talks Let Yours Shout Victory'. The sign urged us to buy national savings certificates, the money was put towards paying for the enormous cost of the war effort which would require untold millions of pounds to buy the

destroyers, bombers, tanks and fighter planes which would one day bring us victory. And millions were invested in war bonds, though many a grumble would be heard after the war about their low rates of interest and the eternity which would elapse before they could be redeemed after the defeat of the Germans and Japanese.

Not that there seems to be much hope of victory, nor indeed fear of defeat, evident in this scene; the woman sitting down beneath Prince Albert is simply taking a no doubt well earned rest from shopping whilst other folk in the picture stroll with apparent unconcern across the roads amongst the sparse traffic. Perhaps the scene would have been busier a little earlier; petrol rationing introduced at the very outbreak of the war in September 1939 had quickly reduced the volume of private traffic. Whether at peace or war however back then we could all enjoy a cigarette without fear for our health. 'Players Please Everyone' would be an advertising slogan which would long remain a familiar sight above Salmon & Gluckstein's tobacconists shop.

Above: A work of art designed to accommodate works of art. The Art Gallery, in Lichfield Street, was the inspiration of Birmingham architect, Julius Chatwin. It is like an Italian Palace with its balustrade, its beautiful sculptured murals and pillars. It is of the highest quality. The Gallery opened in 1884. It was paid for by an anonymous donation of five thousand pounds; this must have seemed an enormous sum at the time. The generous benefactor turned out to be a local builder and businessman, Philip Horsman. He is thanked and remembered by the grateful people of Wolverhampton who built the fountain, in the garden next to the Gallery, in his honour. Constructed of granite and Portland stone, and decorated with dolphins and cupids, it was unveiled in 1896.
Once the garden was surrounded by iron railings, which were taken 'to help with the war effort'. Many people throughout the country returned home from a night out to discover hot molten stumps where their railings had once stood. No one objected to an opportunity 'to do their bit'. They willingly gave up their pots and aluminium pans for scrap. 'Give your scrap to help end the scrap', was the slogan of the time. They would have been saddened to know that little of that which was collected was ever used. The good thing was, however, that it gave a boost to morale, to think that they were bringing the day when their men folk would return, a little closer. In recent years the railings have been replaced.

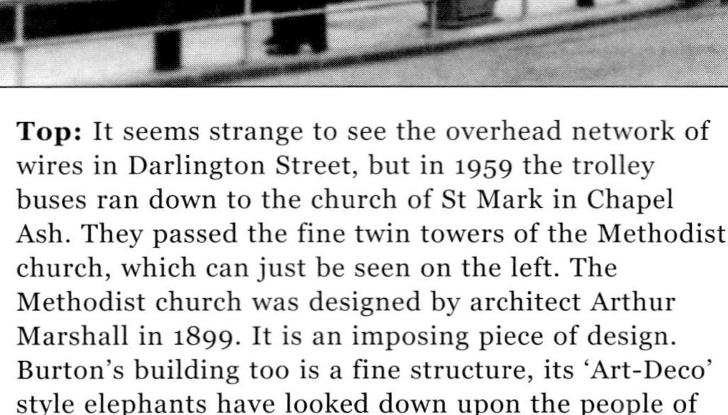

Top: It seems strange to see the overhead network of wires in Darlington Street, but in 1959 the trolley buses ran down to the church of St Mark in Chapel Ash. They passed the fine twin towers of the Methodist church, which can just be seen on the left. The Methodist church was designed by architect Arthur Marshall in 1899. It is an imposing piece of design. Burton's building too is a fine structure, its 'Art-Deco' style elephants have looked down upon the people of the city throughout a war and the austere times which

followed, to the days when the ever increasing number of cars on the road, bore witness to the age of the consumer. They saw the birth of a new section of society, they were called 'teenagers'. A new doll appeared in the shop windows, it was called 'Barbie'. Who could have believed that this toy would become a collector's item, or make its creator, Ruth Hadler, into a lady multi-millionaire? She and her husband founded Mattel toys.

Parked at the side of the road is a Morris Minor. In two short years after the photographer took this picture, the millionth one was built. It was the first British car to reach that target. Designed by Alexander Issigonis it cost £417 in 1959, but in this year a new champion was introduced to the world, the Mini. Designed by the same man and destined to become the darling of the sixties. It would win rallies, carry the shopping, become a fashion statement and, decorated with psychedelic rainbows and flowers, a symbol of sixties 'flower power'.

HERBERT WA
CRADDOCKS' FOR BOOTS
Reade Brothers
EXPRESS POWDERS
CE'S BREAD
BEST OF ALL
&CO

Because it is now such a rare sight, we will begin by looking at the gentleman posing in the foreground. Will the reader please explain to any children, who may be casting their eyes over this picture, that he is, indeed, a policeman! Long, long ago they were required to stand in the middle of the road and direct the traffic. Some even patrolled the streets answering the questions, and giving reliable information such as the time of day. Songs were written about them. 'If you want to know the time - ask a policeman!' advised one song. 'You can't trust the specials like the old time coppers!' warned another. Soon the amount of cars would reach a number where they could not cope and the pressure would be on to find a robotic solution to the problem of traffic. Meantime, in the 1920s, the crowds of shoppers in Victoria Street could spill out onto the road, and there were no lines marked on the road surface to restrict the car. Beattie's flagpoles were a permanent feature. In 1921 they may well have flown flags to celebrate the fiftieth anniversary of the Bank Holidays Act. A better reason, many people who suffered with diabetes would think, would be to fly them to celebrate the isolation of insulin by two Canadian scientists, Charles Best and Frederick Banting.
Posters shout about Craddock's boots, from the side of a passing tram, in competition with those available from the well-established Tyler's Boot shop next to Beatties.

Above: The history books say that the first appeared in London's Piccadilly in 1925, but Wulfrunians may well contest that point. Experimental lights had been tried at this junction in Princes Square and permanent ones were fitted in 1928. A Wolverhampton newspaper reported, in 1929, the case of a Birmingham man who was fined £1 for negligent driving. He had passed a red light in Victoria Street. He said, in his defence, that he had never seen an automatic signal before, even though he drove five hundred miles per week. 'Wolverhampton is ahead of other towns with automatic signals,' remarked the defendant's solicitor, 'We have none in Birmingham, unfortunately.' If he found the traffic lights confusing, quite what he would have made of the instruction on this traffic island, 'Turning right keep right', heaven only knows. He is lucky that he did not have to take the driving test; which was not introduced until 1934.

The first traffic lights, like the continental ones had two colours, red and green. Hence the need to place the small sign which can be seen beneath the signals which reads, 'Move only on green'. At first there was a policeman on duty, in addition to the lights themselves. This was followed by manual override of the lights at busy times, operated by a policeman. When this photograph was taken, in the thirties, they were considered reliable enough to be left on their own, and drivers had become more accustomed to them.

The Westminster Bank building has changed little since extensive refurbishment was carried out in 1930. The London Paperhanging Stores was also given a face-lift at the same time. The workers here would not have believed that their premises would one day be occupied by a business called 'Revolution', spelt with 'e' the wrong way round!

Far right: Standing on the corner of Princes Square looking towards the Art Gallery having, maybe, enjoyed a lunch at the London Restaurant, these gentlemen may well be debating the state of the country. Standing, as they are, with their hands in their pockets. A passer by may well hear the sound of copper coins rattling. Amongst the coins there may be a large 'bun' penny, portraying the head of a young Queen Victoria. So called because her hair was tied in a 'bun'. It is likely that there are some ha'pennies with a galleon under full sail, or the pretty little Farthing displaying the wren. It is the thirties, so amongst the rattling coins may well be that strange newcomer, the twelve-sided three-penny bit. For

The Royal London Mutual Insurance Society proclaims its name to the world, from Princes Square, with confidence. The solid building assures security and reliability. It was built to last. Beyond it is the George Hotel, which, like the Westminster Bank, which stands on the corner where the lady with the pram is attempting to cross, underwent a major rebuilding programme in 1930 and has remained pretty well the same up to the present day. Eyebrows would have gone up, and continued going up, if, in 1930, the suggestion been made that the exclusive George Hotel would some day be renamed the 'Varsity'. Trolley-bus wires are now visible at this busy junction, and the amazing new traffic lights control the flow. One of the favourite pastimes for the men, it seems, is leaning on the rails and watching the world go by. Perhaps they had nothing else better to do, for the economy was unstable, and unemployment was high. Although the electric ovens and vacuum cleaners were available to make the home more comfortable, they may not have been able to afford them. The posters in the windows of the Great Western Railway offices, or the LMS Railway premises on the corner, told them of exotic places where they could get the benefit of the healthy ozone, away from the smoke of the towns. Great sacrifices were made to afford an annual holiday leaving little money for afternoon tea at the London Restaurant. Wouldn't it have been nice to be able to enjoy 'tea with muffins and lashings of butter', so popular with Enid Blyton's 'Famous Five'.

a boy or girl to be given that lovely coin the half-crown for their birthday, or before they set off to the seaside, was a great treat. The things it could buy, or the cinemas it would let you into, or the fairground rides it could pay for, could not be listed on the pages of this book. One could go to the cinema to see Johnny Weissmuller, the new 'Tarzan of the Apes', and still have money to buy enough sweets to make you ill. The half-crown was two shillings and six-pence in value (twelve and a half pence in modern coins of the realm). Far better than receiving a Florin (worth two shillings) for it was a larger and more impressive coin bearing a royal coat of arms and had weight to give it a greater sense of worth.

'Go to it!' is the wartime message from Herbert Morrison the Home Secretary. The women left behind when their men were called to war did precisely that! They kept the wheels of industry turning. When the government launched a campaign to encourage them to 'Go to it', they were overwhelmed by the response from the women of Britain. The ladies operated lathes, produced ammunition for the guns. They worked on the land and clipped tickets on the bus, and delivered the daily 'pinta' needed to answer the call to 'Choose foods that keep you fit'. They were pleased to do the work for every little saved, be it money in a National Savings account or waste paper, would, they hoped, bring their sons, brothers and husbands home a little quicker. It is now thought that we were never healthier as a nation than we were during the war. Many kept hens, answered the call to 'Dig for Victory' by growing their own vegetables, and, with the blockade of the Atlantic by German U-boats preventing the delivery of unhealthy sugar, the diet was basic but sound. The children received their vitamin C in the orange juice distributed at school, and their calcium in the daily bottle of milk. But we did miss our bananas didn't we? Or did we? Many children did not know how to open them when they did get them after the war, and they surprised their parents when they did not particularly like them. Many companies donated money to buy weapons, groups collected sufficient for a machine gun, or even a bomb. Towns paid for a Spitfire, or even a submarine or a ship, and had it named after them. Wolverhampton certainly responded and 'Went to it!'

Right: Standing on the corner, where Victoria Street and Salop Street meet is H Cohen tailor, clothier, and outfitter. This 1927 building, built in brick with a white rendered face, is typical of its period. The block's simple lines were the height of fashion for the year. What an exciting time it was: Charles Lindburgh had flown the Atlantic and landed his aeroplane, 'The Spirit of St Louis', at Croydon before travelling on to Paris in 1927. Cars had to have speedometers from this year forward. What will they think of next? There seemed to be no end to these progressive ideas. Who knows? The lady posing under Cohen's window shade might even be given equal pay one day! Before you could say, 'Change the crystal set for a radio at Lloyds', they had been given the vote from the age of twenty-one, just like the men. This picture must have been taken in the mid to late thirties. By then crossings marked by studs, had been introduced, and the speed limit had been set at thirty miles per hour. Traffic lights, which had first appeared in 1914, were now becoming a common sight. At first they were manually operated by a policeman, but were now 'robotic'. The Guy built trolley buses were now running on several routes around Wolverhampton.

As a building this block has remained virtually unchanged since the day it opened, it is a good example of the best of its day. Cohen the tailor has gone and the shop is now occupied by 'The Red House' fashions.

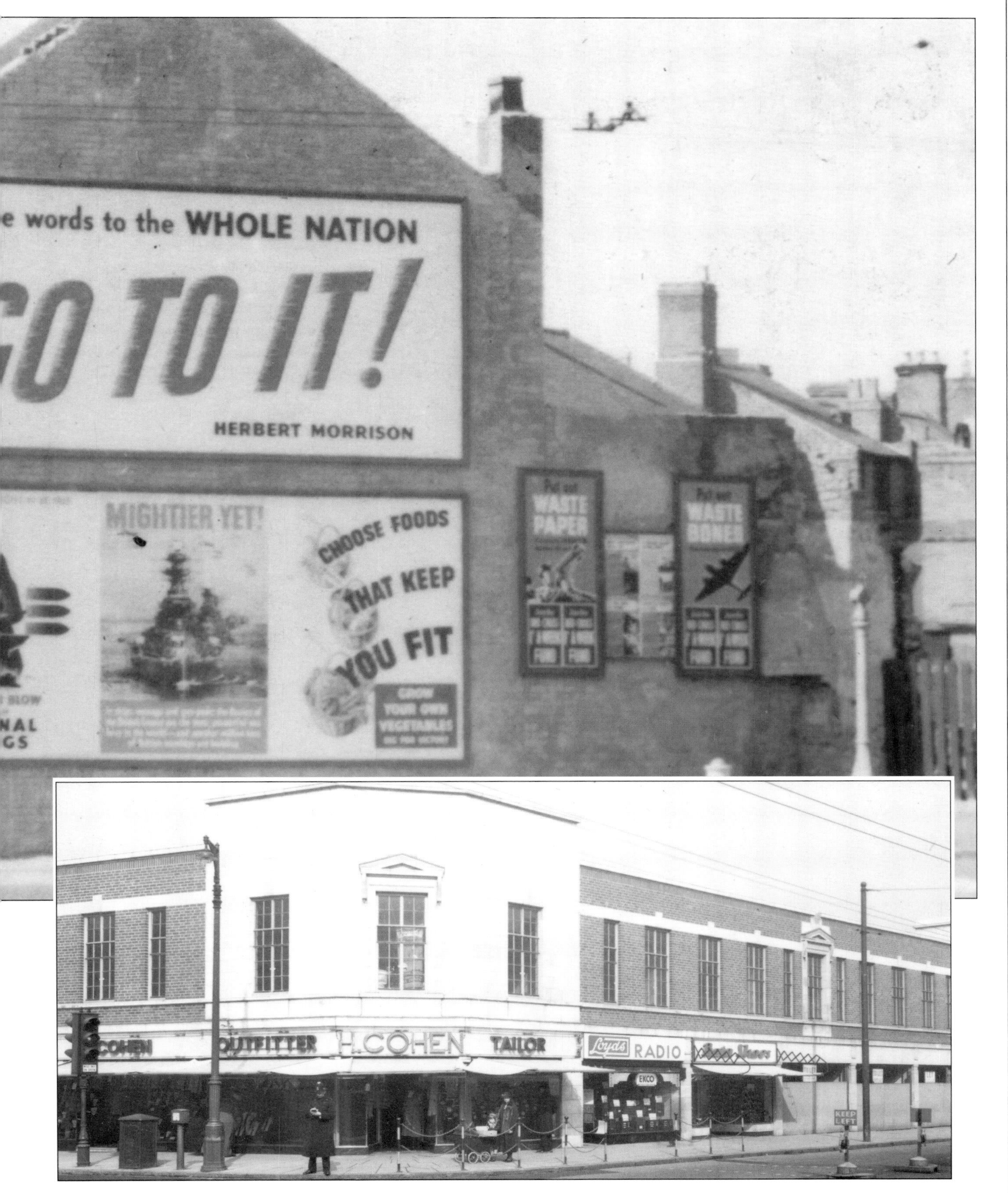
e words to the WHOLE NATION
O TO IT!
HERBERT MORRISON
MIGHTIER YET!
CHOOSE FOODS THAT KEEP YOU FIT
GROW YOUR OWN VEGETABLES
Put out WASTE PAPER
COHEN
OUTFITTER
H. COHEN
TAILOR
Loyds
RADIO
EKCO
KEEP LEFT

Left: The boys are shouting invitations to the girls to meet them. 'Meet where?' comes back the question. 'By the lamppost of course!' is the obvious reply. Lampposts served the purpose given to the market cross in the Middle Ages - it acted as a focal point around which to meet. It was more socially acceptable than standing outside a public house, like the Holly Bush in Moore Street. Long before 1950, when this photograph was taken, George Formby had leaned against one 'in case a certain little lady passed by'. We can all remember those places that meant little to anyone else, but at times in our lives they were the

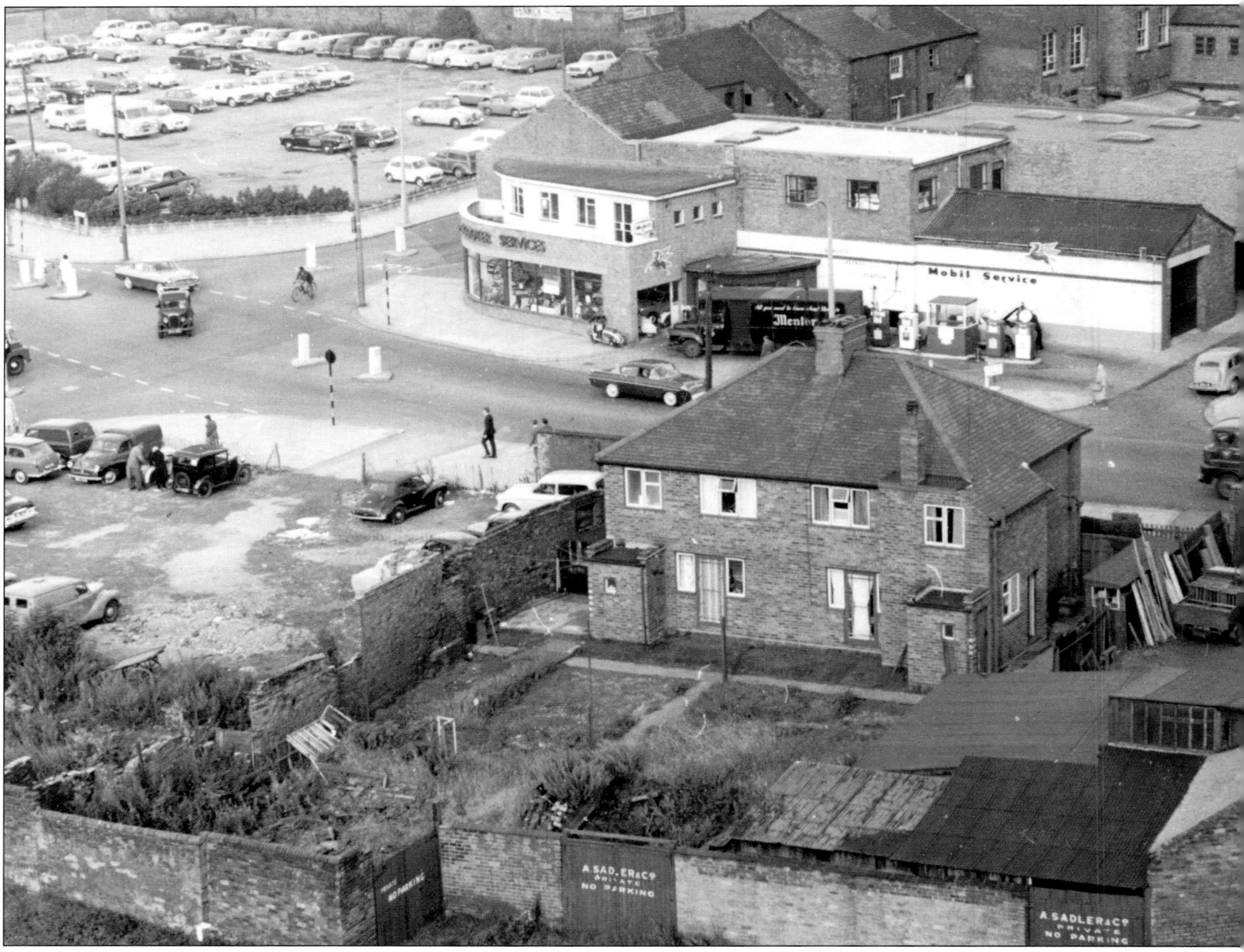

centre of the universe. It may have been the corner of a street, or beneath the Prince's statue, or our favourite coffee bar, the Milano. It may well have been outside the Penn Cinema for the second house, or 'Meet you inside!' was the call if the young man couldn't afford to pay for two tickets. In 1950 it was expected that the boys would pay and look after the girls (these times were the pinnacle of chauvinism). Their male pride was slightly dented if the girl offered to pay her own way. These were the days when girls played with prams and the boys played with lead soldiers. Isn't it surprising how time has changed attitudes.
This housing had been built for miners and factory workers. Much of it had deteriorated into little more than a slum. Between the two world wars 8,822 houses and 25 shops were built by Wolverhampton council. Of these 3,736 were specifically for the slum clearance project. Flats and houses were erected at Tettenhall, Wednesfield and Siesden, with the agreement of the then separate councils.

Below left: This semi-detached fortress stands ready to defend itself against the oncoming ring road. Isolated on an island now, soon many changes will come about in the name of progress, but the stout walls, which already show the scars of previous battles, will try to keep out the invaders. Warnings shout in vain from painted signs on the castle gates telling of the dire consequences of even the thought of parking outside the gates of Sadler and Company. From the upstairs windows, the enemy camp can be seen, or is it simply the market stalls on the Brickkiln Patch?
The enemy are cars, whose numbers grow daily, create chaos and mayhem, and the town must give way to their demands. Already they park on spare land as if to claim it for their own. In 1963 the ring road will sweep down from the Penn roundabout to Salop Street taking away everything in its' path. Once there was a market, which lay safely wrapped in the shadow of the St Peter's Church, but it too had to make way for change. Alongside there stood a permanent market building in Cheapside, but, despite its' ingenious Victorian design, it also disappeared.
In 1963 it was not only Sadler and Company that was under threat, but an entire railway network throughout the country. The man wielding an axe was the famous Dr Beeching. This is a name that sent terror down the spines of children - and engine drivers. He closed half of all the railway stations, and the majority of branch lines throughout the land.

Bottom: On a grey day shortly after the war, workmen repair the surface of the road on Brickkiln Patch. There are no prizes for an explanation as to how this road got its name. It has seen many industries come and go over the years. It has seen the bustle and excitement of market stalls and fairgrounds. It has also seen the craft of the metal worker. Some of the metal work wrought in the lane has been decorative and artistic, but some was most unpleasant. Henry Waldram, of Brickkiln Lane, made handcuffs and iron collars for the slave traders.
On a more cheerful note, however, they did not know how to make wheel clamps, and so the cars may continue to enjoy free parking. The caravan probably is the living accommodation for the driver of the steamroller, or for the men who are laying power cables for the new concrete lampposts, a new and exciting shape at the time that invoked much debate. This simple, functional design has now become so accepted that it is now hardly noticed. Our modern eye would be attracted by its' cast iron predecessor. The lady making her way down the road to the shops would find a queue, for goods were still scarce and many still rationed. Perhaps she can forget those mundane problems with a trip to the Odeon. About this time John Gregson was racing his vintage car 'Genevieve, to London Bridge, and although he did not win the race, he did win the heart of the fair lady, Kay Kendal.

Events & occasions

No-one gives the Prince Consort even a glance as he sits forever gazing beyond the railings into the public conveniences in Queen's Square in 1935. As he watches he must be in awe of the march of progress going on around him. His beloved Victoria has been dead for over thirty years. Edward too is gone, and now George has been king for twenty-five years. It seems impossible to believe that this is George's Silver Jubilee, hence the red, white and blue bunting which waves in the breeze above his head. Doesn't time fly when you're made of bronze and have nowhere to go?
The toilets, into which he looks, are among the first in the land to provide facilities for the ladies as well as the men. Quite how they coped before we shudder to think.
The conveniences were built in 1902 for the benefit of visitors to the Art and Industries Exhibition held in Wolverhampton at the time. They were discreetly camouflaged behind shrubs. No modest lady would want anyone to know where she was going. But these are the bold thirties when women could vote at the age of twenty-one, the same as the men. (If the reader takes a careful look at the prince, you will possibly see him shudder in surprise at such a progressive idea.)
These cars parked outside Althams had better take care, for this was the year that an American idea crept into Britain - the Parking Meter! It seems poetic justice that amongst the first ones to be introduced to our shores were placed outside the American Embassy in London.

Above: There is a slight breeze to move the flags patriotically declaring the love of the people for their Monarch on his Jubilee in 1935. The photographer steadies his camera in the third floor window of Lloyds Bank overlooking Queen's Square. The bunting to the right of the shot is attached to the roof of the Queen's Picture House. The well-known mock timbered building on the opposite corner was once The Shakespeare public house. Later it became the premises of B & B Jeweller's. Surrounded by flags, and separated by the royal coat of arms, are the portraits of King George V and his Queen, Mary.

The Hippodrome in Wolverhampton is unique. That peculiar onion shaped dome on top of a tower is so distinctive. The architect took a flight of fancy and created a fairy-tale building, and which, it tells without speaking, of the variety to be found within. It is as fanciful as any stage set, and as inspired as the Brighton Pavilion.

Advancing up the street there appears to be a vehicle of the kind that was favoured by the railway companies. A useful flat backed truck, with a single seat, open sided, cab at the front over a single wheel. Highly manoeuvrable, these trucks could turn within their own length. An asset in a goods yard or station where space was restricted. They were, however, slow and more than a little unstable when detached from their trailer.

Bunting was strung across all of the streets of the town, as well as here in Dudley Street, when George V celebrated his Silver Jubilee in 1935. His portrait looks down upon a loyal Wolverhampton from a banner, which declares the rejoicing. He was a much-loved monarch, and, reportedly a modest and pleasant gentleman.

By now there was little disguising Hitler's intention to build a formidable fighting force. He announced his intentions to increase the size of Germany's navy and create a flotilla of submarines. Herman Goering announced the intention to increase the number in the army to four times that allowed under the terms of the Treaty of Versailles. By now the treaty was not worth the paper it was written on. The British government went ahead with its plans to build up the strength of the Royal Air Force. New technology was needed also and, in 1935, scientists and engineers developed a technique for detecting the presence of aeroplanes. It was called Radio Detection And Ranging, better known by the initials RADAR. Very soon engineering companies in Wolverhampton were busy on this task. Boulton Paul were making the 'Defiant' fighter planes. Guy Motor Company, under the leadership of Sir William Lyons, developed the technology to weld armour plating to produce a waterproof seam. Prior to their accomplishing this feat joints had been held with rivets. They built light armoured vehicles, the four-wheel drive Quad Ant, and, reputedly, an armoured command post vehicle for Field Marshall Montgomery.

Dobbin to the rescue! He will provide the royal coach for the children of Tettenhall as they join the Coronation parade. A new Elizabethan era has begun. No school today. We were all given a mug with the Queen's portrait on it, and a copy of the New Testament with EIIR embossed on the dark blue cover in gold. Quite what the costumes were supposed to represent is not clear. The lad with an umbrella may be a Charlie Chaplin, or another character who appeared both on film and in the comics, Stan Laurel.

Such dates are always present in the local pub quiz. In what year were there three monarchs on the throne of England? The answer is, of course, 1936. King George V died at the beginning of the year, Edward succeeded him

but abdicated and was followed by his brother, George VI. And now Elizabeth II became queen in 1952, and was crowned in June 1953. One question that was probably asked on this day is, 'Do we all stand when the National Anthem is played?' We always did, even at the cinema when the film had ended. Though, in honesty, there was a dash for the exit as the titles rolled. But, if the first chord struck up before we had made it to the exit, we stood respectfully as we had always been taught.

At the end of the day it was home for a mug of Ovaltine or 'sleep sweeter with Bourn-vita'. And what was that brown tonic, which mother brought out of the kitchen cupboard? She insisted that it was good for us as we were made to swallow a spoonful - was it called Virol?

Above: If you stand in Princess Street with your back to the 'Tap and Spile' Public House, as the photographer did in 1937, you will see that there have been a few minor changes over the years. The decorations, to celebrate the coronation of George VI, have long since been wrapped and put away, and an upholstery firm now occupies the Counties Libraries premises. The clock now has a white dial with black hands, but still ticks away the time to make sure that the people of Wolverhampton are punctual for their appointments, provided that they are not tempted to call at the Talbot Inn next door to the library. The more temperate in 1937 may have been lured by a call to join the library scheme for the princely sum of 2d per book per week. This building had only opened four years earlier, in 1933, the year when a certain Herr Adolph Hitler had become Chancellor of Germany. No one gave much thought to the possible consequences of his party's policies. Some respected statesmen in this country thought that the appointment was 'a necessary one for the good of Germany'. George V had died and Edward VIII had been crowned king. He abdicated because the woman he loved was a divorcee and was not considered 'suitable' as queen. His brother, Prince Albert, took the crown, but wished to be known as George VI. This shy man, who suffered all his life from a nervous stutter. He and his wife, now known throughout the world as the Queen Mother, were well liked and warmly accepted by the country.

Inset: It was in 1877 that James Beattie first opened the Victoria Drapery Store in Victoria Street. As the store grew it extended into the premises of F W Bradford, and Jeanette's Fashions. The whole of the facade underwent a major face-lift to project the right image for a department store with ambitions for the future. When Victoria Street was widened, it gave a better view of the impressive building. In 1992 they acquired the corner premises of Burtons Tailors.

Tastefully draped with swags of red, white and blue, the store rejoices in the coronation of the young Queen Elizabeth. As Princess Elizabeth she had been married only a few years earlier, and she and her husband, Prince Phillip, took on many of the duties of the king who was terminally ill with cancer. His left lung had had to be removed in 1951 and, whilst the Princess was away in Kenya in his place, he died at Sandringham. It was the Duke of Edinburgh who had the sad duty of giving her the news.

During 1953 the people gathered around their radios, for it was still only the wealthy who owned a television, and waited for the popular 'What's my line?' quiz game. The panel had now gained a new member. She was the young, 33 year old Lady Isabel Barnett, whose wit and charm made her very popular with the listeners. Despite the increase in sales due to the televising of the entire coronation, they were still very much a luxury item. Those entering the post office to buy a television licences as well as a radio licence made heads turn in envy.

Top right: There was only a year between the decorations and the bunting going up on Wolverhampton's Town Hall for the Jubilee of George V, and the coronation of his son Prince Albert, who decided that he wished to be known as George VI. The romance between Edward VIII and Mrs Wallis Simpson is well chronicled. There was considerable concern about his suitability to be king, not only because many found it hard to accept a divorcee as queen, but also because of their lifestyle, and their socialising with many in positions of power within Germany. The Germans had by now made it clear that they were building their navy, and their army. Many atrocities were being committed against the Jews. It was a difficult time requiring all public figures to be tactful and diplomatic in all things. Edward announced his intention to abdicate, as he did not feel that he could discharge his duties without the help of the woman he loved by his side. As his brother met with the accession council, he slipped quietly away from Portsmouth aboard HMS Fury.

These were difficult times, when men marched the length of England to demand the right to work and earn a satisfactory wage. The average family needed six pounds per week to stay above the poverty line. The average in fact was only two pounds per week. Public attention may well have been on the build up of forces in Germany, the social problems at home, the abdication of Edward, and the accession of King George VI, but suddenly the life of a ten-year-old girl changed dramatically, for one day she would become Queen Elizabeth II.

All heads are sensibly protected from the sun on 6th May 1935, as people gather in West Park to celebrate the jubilee of a popular monarch, King George V. Some said the king was the epitome of an English gentleman. This is an age when crowds were orderly; they possessed self-discipline, which we have apparently lost over the years. The children are gathered to sing to an audience of doting parents, and the band strikes up to lead them through their programme. No doubt some patriotic music was played at this time, when Britain was gearing up to prepare for a possible war with Germany. In the distance the gasworks can be seen. In any other town gas works are places of little interest, but in Wolverhampton strange things could happen at the gas works. In 1882 a balloon, filled with coal gas, was launched from the Molineux Gardens. It was a Hudson's Soap war balloon, which was piloted by a certain Captain Morton, and Colonel Thornycroft of Tettenhall. It was a facsimile of those used by the military in South Africa. The gas was piped directly from the Stafford Road gas-works. Attached by cable to a winch powered by a traction engine, it rose to a height of a thousand feet, which was thought to be a world altitude record at the time. Members of the public were charged ten shillings each for a ride in the balloon. That was a considerable sum in 1882. Perhaps they were not so crazy after all!

At leisure

It is the 7th July 1956 when the children from Holy Trinity Church, Ettingshall, Sunday school, pose for the Dudley Herald cameraman. Do any readers recognise themselves? These were the days when churches and Sunday schools were well attended. When friendships were made that would last a lifetime. There were no worries beyond that of hoping that the half-crown that granny had given you was still wrapped in the knot of your handkerchief, or, in the case of the young lady on the left, in your up-to-the-date snakeskin handbag. Providing that the bus came to collect them and take them to the seaside, or wherever, they didn't care about this doctor called Mr Beeching who was closing all the railways, and a Mr Nasser who, 'my dad says', is trying to take the canal away from us! As far as these little people knew the Suez Canal is just off Millfields Road.

Do you remember your school caps? The moment the corner was turned on the way home from school it folded neatly with the, neb inside, and slipped into the pocket, or it was turned sideways in an act of defiance. How many girls had bonnets crocheted by mum or granny, or a lady who made them for the church summer fair? Pigtails and hair slides. Ribbons tied in a bow like the neat, well-dressed 'Shirley Temple look-alike' on the right. It is not necessary to know the children in this picture to enjoy the day. We had days like this ourselves. How quickly they go, but they only need the slightest nudge to bring them all flooding back.

HIPPODROME
6.15
8.30
CHARLIE KUNZ
ARTHUR PRINCE
LES ALLEN
ROS BEYARD DANCERS
LA PETITE POUPEE
LEN & BILL LOWE
RAYMOND SISTERS AND ALLEN
TUPPY OLIVER
HIPPODROME BAR
BUTLERS ALES
A 454 WALSALL
A 449 STAFFORD
A 460
BASS

Hippodrome once meant a circus or a place where chariots raced. The word 'hippo' means 'horse'. There have never been any reports of chariots racing here but many well known artists have 'trod the boards' at Wolverhampton's Hippodrome. They had ranged from the Lancashire Nightingale, Gracie Fields, to opera singers. Some were lesser known. Who was 'La Petite Poopee'? What act did she perform? Whatever happened to Tuppy Oliver? Charlie Kunz, that wizard of the piano, whose sheet music and 78 records were so popular, is appearing in person. The bar is serving Butler's popular beer in the bar on this day in the late 50s. Today it houses a Wine Lodge, but still serves the customers with a pint of beer if they so wish.

Across Queen's Square is the Queen's Picture House. How many of us rushed to the Saturday morning pictures, having worried all week about how Flash Gordon was going to escape from the gas chamber, where he had been trapped by the evil Emperor Ming. The school boy who shouted the word 'Shazam' and, in a puff of smoke turned into Captain Marvel, kept us fascinated because he did not turn into a cartoon, as Superman did, every time he had to fly. We shuffled in our seats and were shouted at by the usherette if we became too noisy when Roy Rogers burst into song. That was the trouble with the 'goodies'; they always got the girl and had to win her heart by singing soppy cowboy songs.

Below: There are still traces of the camouflage on the roofs of the airport buildings and the hut in the foreground, but there is no threat on this day in 1948. The football match can go ahead on the sports ground alongside Pendeford Airport. Ten years earlier, on 25th June 1938, the airport had opened on part of the Barnhurst Farm site. The Goodyear Trophy Air Race was held here and it attracted pilots from all over the country to compete for the prestigious award. It was attended by, amongst others, the well-known female aviatrix Amy Johnson.
The land adjacent to this had been given to the aircraft manufacturer Boulton Paul, with rights to fly there for one hundred years! The government realised that, the possibility of a war was a real one and that the aeroplane would play a very important part in the conflict. Boulton Paul built 2,198 aircraft during their time, the most successful of these being their own designed 'Defiant' fighter. Although it never gained the legendary reputation gained by the Spitfire it was considered to be one of the most successful fighter planes during the winter of 1940/1941. The company also made gun turrets for other aircraft, as well as working on the famous 'Canberra'. After the war they converted Wellington bombers for peacetime use. In 1961 they merged to form Dowty Boulton Paul. In 1990 the company was known as Dowty Aerospace making components for spacecraft. In 1950 another celebrity competed in the King's Cup Air Race, his name was Group Captain Peter Townsend. He and Princess Margaret wanted to marry but the romance came to an end in 1955 with an announcement from the Princess that, because he was a divorcee, she had decided not to marry him, even though she could have done so in a civil ceremony. Although the crowds flocked to see the air displays, they did not use the airport in large numbers and it closed in 1971.

Three times a year in some years, from 1939 to 1959, Pat Collins brought his Fair to Brickkiln Patch. In 1960 the construction of the new market meant a change of venue to site just off Broad Street, and later to Falklands Street car park, and even later still it was held in the main parks.

Having passed through the archway, the smells and sounds competed with each other for your attention. Music blared and vendors cried out. You could throw the darts and win a cuddly toy, drop the ping-pong ball into the jam jar, or catch a yellow plastic duck floating by on an endless river. The sound of the 'Wonderland' fairground organ filled the air. The organ was first seen on the market patch in 1908. We watched as the candy-floss machine spun sugar into fine pink strands. With a deft flick and twist of the wrist, it was collected onto a stick and handed over. It melted away magically in the mouth. Then the smell of hotdogs and onions came next. Having devoured one we were ready to visit the Wall of Death. We watched the stomach churning antics of the rider, as his motorcycle defied gravity. The rider was held to the wall of the pit by the centrifugal force as his noisy bike circled. Girls screamed when he wobbled near to the edge. The boys always knew that it was just part of the act. Perhaps it was Wolverhampton's own daredevil stuntman who went under the name of Jerry-de-Roy.

In the 1930s the imposing offices of the London Mutual Insurance Society dominated Prince's Square. Despite the relatively small number of vehicles on the road, at the time this photo was taken, Prince's Square was nevertheless, even in those far off days, a busy junction at peak times.

That this photograph was taken in Summer is clearly evident from the strong shadows and the awnings pulled down over the shop windows. Prominent amongst those businesses is W Snape whose tea and coffee shop would be renowned amongst locals. Snapes would later move to Queen Street where customers could continue to go to have their tea weighed out in the same way it had been for decades.

The most important feature of the scene however is neither the London Mutual's office nor the fascinating old cars we can see, but the traffic lights.

Prince's Square reputedly had the very first set of traffic lights in England installed in 1928, they appeared in Wolverhampton even before they did in its larger neighbour Birmingham. The lights in the photograph are however not the original set. These are mounted in the middle of the Square on a pole; the first lights were suspended from cables above the roadway.

The unfamiliar equipment undoubtedly caused confusion and in addition to having the first traffic lights Wolverhampton also had the dubious distinction of being amongst the first towns to fine a motorist for running through a red light. The unfortunate motorist was fined £1.

On the move

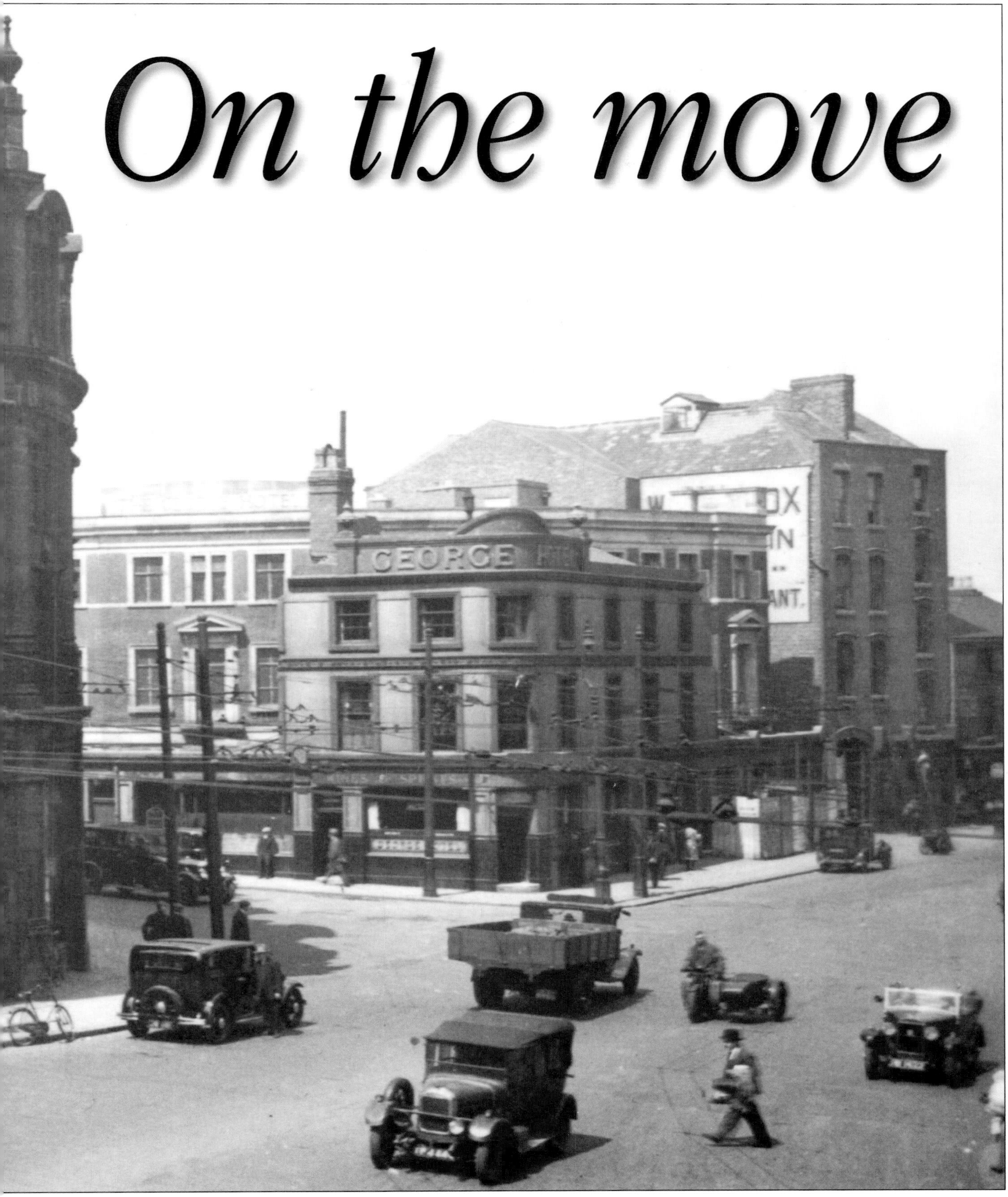

Cyril Dobbs, the Chief Engineer, standing to the left of the picture has chosen his spot in the picture with care. Smart in its apple green and primrose yellow paintwork, and sporting the coat of arms of Wolverhampton on the bonnet, vehicle number 214 undergoes the statutory tilt test. Edwin Wilton, who was the Technical Assistant at Wolverhampton Corporation, stands between the other two colleagues. The top deck was loaded with sand bags. The unladen weight was increased from 8 tons 3cwt to a test weight of 11 tons 18 cwt in the upper deck. The lower salon received a weight equal to that of the driver and the conductor only. Then the bus was tilted. These men must have known exactly what they were dong, but it looks terribly dangerous even though necessary! The bus in the background was built for service in Durban, South Africa. At a council meeting held in March 1961, the decision was taken to abandon the trolley bus in favour of motorbuses. The route bound trolleys had reached the point where they had reached the end of their useful lives and all needed replacing. An order of that size would take a number of years to fill, during which time motor buses would have to be hired to 'fill the gaps' in the service. They were much more expensive to buy, and the cost of renewal, and extension of the overhead wires to serve the new housing areas swung the decision towards their gradual phasing out. In truth the traffic had become heavier, and the constant stop-start driving caused them to become 'dewired' and the trolley heads to be damaged. The old friends had to go!

6

Above: Many will remember running to catch the last bus home after a night dancing. Or maybe running when legs, and other parts, ached, from circling the rink at the Roller Dome on Temple Street. At the height of its popularity a maple wood floor, set on a bitumen base, had replaced the original floor and the skates became much quieter. The music did not have to be played at such a high volume. It was then that the name changed to 'Whispering Wheels'. Many a romance began on the last bus home. 'See you on the last bus', was a common cry amongst the teenagers. Invented in the 50s, teenagers became a social 'problem'. Bill Haley and the Comets caused riots in cinemas, to such a degree that many local authorities banned the film. We did not think we were living in special times but Harold Macmillan, the Prime Minister, told us we had never had it so good, and maybe we hadn't!

By the time those cheeky chaps, the Beatles, with the strange haircuts had entered the music scene from their native Liverpool, trolley buses were reaching the end of their service in Wolverhampton. There were many new housing developments and the cost of extending the network of electric power lines would have been too expensive to serve them all. Most of the buses needed replacing but trolley buses were much more costly than the equivalent diesel driven motorbus. The trolley became disconnected from the cables frequently with the stop-start driving required as traffic increased. These route-bound, smoothly accelerating, carriages slipped into the history books. But before we say good-bye, let us take one last look at these trolley-buses outside the Park Lane depot, for they were elegant, aesthetically pleasing, works of art. Very smart in their apple green and primrose yellow paintwork.

Five magnificent vehicles, waxed and polished to a high shine, their chrome plating gleaming in the sun, are posing proudly for the camera here in Molineux Street. Bob and his taxis were a familiar sight in Wolverhampton, and slowly his business grew. GDA 113 was new to Bob in 1948. He, and his fellow chauffeurs, took pride in their cars, and offered that opportunity for a little luxury in our lives. When settled on the leather seats in the back of these carriages we felt like royalty. Suddenly our backs straightened and we posed, and the problems of a world recovering from a war disappeared. Ration books were quickly forgotten. It was escapism of the very best kind. The war had been over for three years, but the country was still very poor. Bread

rationing did not cease until the end of July 1948.
Such cars had character and personality, and we gave them individual names. Even the manufacturer gave them names like 'Princess'. They glided away with the depression of the accelerator like the elegant thoroughbreds that they undoubtedly were. They were stable and safe on their heavy chassis. Doors closed with a solid clunk. Wood trimmed the inside giving a feel of craftsmanship and opulence. These were the days when a car was loved and cherished.
Orville Wright died in 1948. He, and his brother, had successfully got an aeroplane to fly; even if it was only a few feet from the ground. By 1948, aeroplanes had been used to deadly effect in a way that Orville could never have imagined.

Top: The last trolley bus in Wolverhampton ran in 1967 whilst the building of the Wulfrun Centre, seen under construction here in the background, began in 1966 neatly providing a useful method of dating this picture taken of Snow Hill.
On the right is the Gaumont cinema opened in 1932 and built with dressing rooms and a stage in addition to its silver screen to enable it to double as a theatre. The Gaumont closed in 1973, the site eventually became the Wilkinsons store, though not before the cinema had hosted pop concerts featuring such artists as the evergreen Cliff Richard and American rocker Gene Vincent who was to be badly injured in the British car crash in which rock and roll legend Eddie Cochrane would be killed.
In the background is that temple of learning, the Central Library, built to a prize-winning design by architect Henry Hare. The library was opened in 1902 and would provide generations of readers with both education and entertainment. How many readers of this book were addicted to reading in their early years before television dominated the world of childhood? How many eagerly awaited their 'coming of age' when they could gain that passport to the world, their first adult library ticket, though no doubt saying a fond farewell to their childhood favourites? How could we ever forget Biggles and Billy Bunter or the seemingly inexhaustible number of books by Enid Blyton and Richmal Crompton which we all read under the blankets by torchlight long after official 'lights out'?

Above: Proudly on display outside the depot on Cleveland Road stand the gleaming new Guy built trolley buses ready for service between 1927 and 1929. Looking splendid and efficient with their 61-seater Dobson bodies, built on a six-wheeler chassis. The old hospital at the opposite side of the road must have been delighted

that the rattling noisy trams were being replaced by quiet gliding machines. Nothing accelerated so smoothly as the trolley bus. It had no need for gear changing. Only if it had to move or stop violently did the pantograph, that current collector on the end of the two long poles, come away from the overhead wires. The conductor withdrew a long bamboo pole, which had a hook attachment, from a tube beneath the bus. Catching the ring beneath the pantograph he swung it deftly back into position. In winter sparks would often fly as the arm renewed contact with the wire.

The door was newly designed for easier access, and became the standard pattern for many years to come. Young men cultivated the new skill of stylishly hanging onto the rail and then dropping off the platform just before the bus had come to a standstill. They would not attempt the stunt if there were any Inspectors on the bus or waiting at the stop to get on to check the work of the conductor and driver. How many looked exactly like 'Blakey' from the popular television series 'On the buses'? Most of them provided the inspiration for the character with their attitude of total power!

PRODUCTS
MARKS
Crown WALLPAPERS
BOF 879
568

Number 568, seen here parked outside Marks and Spencer Ltd., in Market Street, is a Guy single-decker bus. It was one of a number of the same design originally made to seat 34 people, this one was converted to 24 seats, to give sufficient standing space for an additional 26 passengers. The first five buses of this model, numbers 561 to 565, were delivered in 1949. Number 561 remained long after the others were withdrawn from public passenger service, and was used as a snowplough!

The weather must have been cold on this day in the early fifties. The bus is wearing a rolled down cover over the engine radiator. When it was pulled over the radiator, it allowed the engine to reach the optimum working temperature more quickly. Those car drivers, who could not afford the purpose-made radiator blankets, would cut a piece of card to the right size, and insert it between the grill and the radiator in order to achieve the same effect. There was always the problem, however, that, if the engine did not fire into action with the first turns of the starter motor, it had to be cranked by hand. This meant that the card had to be removed again to allow the cranking handle to pass through. The lever was inserted through the hole, visible in the radiator just above the number plate, and turned by hand. There was a skill in giving it a good swing. Should the engine 'back-fire'; the cranking handle could swing back viciously and deliver a hard smack. Many an internal combustion engine, in those days, had a malicious, spiteful attitude, and an aggressive personality. Those drivers, who did not take careful note of the temperature gauge reading, and stop to remove the cover from the radiator when the required working temperature had been achieved, risked the problem of overheating. Those were the golden years of motoring!

Keep Left says the sign in letters so large that one immediately supposes it was placed there in the days before a sight check was a compulsory part of the driving test.
The roundabout with its multiple sign posts surmounted by four lamps and decorative metal work once had pride of place at the junction of Dudley Street and Cleveland Street.
Modern road signs are hard enough to read but motorists travelling on this wet murky afternoon would be forced to slow right down to read the curiously duplicated signs, a symptom of the mix and match approach to updating road signs which was to take many years to complete. Even at the end of the century in a few out of the way places one would still come across these now archaic looking road signs whose scale was intended for a far more leisurely age; try reading something this size when you're zooming past them at sixty miles an hour - forget it!
Traders at the time this photo was taken include CD Nokes on the far left whilst Billinghams, the authorised Ford dealers,is on the right, though there seem to be no examples of either Fords or any other cars on the road as we look down Dudley Street. Quite what the reason for the almost total absence of cars is unfathomable but we know that it is impossible to capture such a scene today anywhere in the United Kingdom such has been the pace of change.

WEST BROMWICH 8¼
BIRMINGHAM 13¼
CANNOCK
STAFFORD
BILLINGHAM
AUTHORISED Ford DEALER

Now a wide, fast lane sweeps through Chapel Ash giving priority to the traffic from the right of the picture. It is interesting to see the things, which have, or have not changed, around St Marks Church. Bank's Brewery is still making excellent beer and continuing to supply the Clarendon Hotel, on the corner, in the shadow of the brewery. The chimney smoking happily in the 60s has disappeared, but the one that seems idle on this day, still remains and has gained a metallic partner in recent years. In the foreground is a red telephone box. Who would have guessed at the time that they would one day acquire antique status and become collectors items. How many remember the days when we inserted the old large copper pennies and waited for a response? As soon as we were connected we pressed button 'A' to be heard, or if there were no reply, button 'B' would return our cash. Little boys always checked to see if the money had been taken when a call had been unsuccessful. It nearly always had!

The bus is now diesel powered with side door access. No longer a platform at the rear onto which an athletic passenger could jump as he caught up to the advancing bus. Soon to become as extinct as the dodo bird, was the bus conductor or conductress. He, or she, were the ones who collected the coppers for the journey and allocated a bus ticket. The 'clippies' they were called. Slung diagonally across their shoulders they would carry the cash bag and the ticket dispenser incorporating a punch to make a hole in your return ticket. Many a schoolboy collected bus tickets and exchanged them in the school playground. They were the currency of the time, along with postage stamps and cigarette cards. They were as valuable to the owner, in their day, as any Pokémon card.

Shopping spree

Once upon a time in a town called Wolverhampton, trams trundled too and fro up and down Victoria Street. For a long time black had been the fashionable colour as a much-loved Queen mourned her beloved Albert. Horses were the main source of transport and Tyler's Boot Market had not given way to Burton's. Neither had Mr J Beattie taken over the property from Burton's. When there was no such thing as a supermarket. When the Maypole Dairy Company, seen on the left with its' row of white glass globed lights, was recently built. It continued serving the people until it was demolished to make way for the redevelopment and the creation of the Mander Centre, many readers might well remember the shop next door trading as 'Adrien', providing the height of fashion to those who could afford it in the fifties. Pedestrians walked where they wished. It was safe chat in the middle of Victoria Street, provided that it was not within the tram lines, though even they moved noisily and slowly enough to warn of their progress. The front and back of the tram was fitted with a guard net, to prevent any person from being run over by the tram wheels. Isn't it easy to romanticise a period in which we did not live? Not all was long skirt and straw hat fashion. At this time, with the introduction of education for all, came the legislation for medical checks to be conducted in schools. Large numbers of children were discovered who required urgent dental treatment, suffered with eye problems, or had a number of diseases caused by poor diet. Many had contracted tubercolosis. We dreaded the day when the school nurse called to examine us for nits, head-lice and ringworm. The shame of it, if you were the one who was sent home with a note because you had head-lice!

Grandmother always had a saying for every situation, or words to lead a happy life. One such piece of advice was, 'Don't walk about with your eyes in the gutter all the time. Lift your head up!' Do so in Dudley Street and, whilst you may collide with other shoppers, you will be surprised how many of these facades have survived the vast number of changes which have occurred. The skyline is a lesson in architectural fashion.

Granny also said, 'Take care of the pennies and the pounds will take care of themselves'. Forever on the lookout for a bargain she was the very kind that F W Woolworth's targeted. In the 1920s they boasted that there was nothing over six-pence in their shop. They knew the difficult times in which the people found themselves and provided a 'bargain'. It was a winning formula, for soon FW had enlisted the help of his brother CS Woolworth, and was soon opening stores in America, Canada and Europe as well as the UK.

Next-door was that well-known Grocer's shop. When money was scarce, shoppers wanted to know that they were buying good quality. They felt sure they would get that at Lipton's. Carefully weighed and served one could buy the finest cheeses, and the best of tea. During the war there were government education films shown at the cinema between the 'B' film and the main attraction. These always brought howls of laughter from the audience when a well-manicured housewife repeated the simplest instructions on how to make a cup of tea, as if she was delivering another ten commandments.

The motorcar is a relatively new phenomenon in the early 20s, and the people wander across the road freely. The rules of the road have not yet been written and drivers move wherever they want or wherever they can. It wasn't until 1927 that roads were marked with white lines to keep control and some sort of order. Did they know that this was such a golden age when the motorist could park his car anywhere he wanted in Queen's Square? There are no clamps, or parking tickets, traffic wardens, or the dreaded yellow lines. On a beautiful day, such as this one, one could drive with the canvas top folded away. And, after enjoying the delights of a horseless carriage, or a motorcycle and sidecar, park it right outside Lyons Café and partake of afternoon tea and scones. This scene is a vintage car collector's dream!

On such a day it is surprising that ice cream, the new import from Italy, is not on sale in the square. 'Penny licks' were popular. It was a lot of money in those days of low pay and high unemployment. But there were those who could afford them. It was the fashion you see! A small conical shaped glass with a shallow indentation in the top had a lick of ice cream deposited on top. Not a lot was given, because it was difficult to make. The ice was expensive to obtain and to keep frozen. Having finished the glass was handed back to the vendor who would wipe it with a cloth, or not wipe it as the case may be, before passing it to the next customer with another measure. Wonderful!

Above: Vernon's Football Pools offered a chance to dream in the austere days of the 40s and 50s. It seemed more sensational to win on the Pools than to win the more spectacular Lottery of today. Life was harder and this was the only way out of a mundane existence for many. Viv Nicholson was one of the successful ones. She went out and bought a pink Cadillac. She said she would, 'Spend, Spend, Spend!' So much so that her tragic life filled the national newspapers, and became the subject of a London musical in the 1990s.

The building supporting the hoarding has now gone as the road along Salop Street has been widened over the years, but the block on the right, housing H Cohen, still remains and looks as 'modern' as it did when it was built in 1927. The driver of Collin's van would be surprised to know that he had arrived at what is now 'Paradise', and, where Blakemores Ltd once provided the groceries, one can now buy a dress from Uma Fashions.

The road surface looks to be in need of urgent attention. The cast iron circular manhole covers rattled alarmingly every time a vehicle ran over them. There were even people who collected them as a hobby, just as others collect stamps. Or more precisely, they took rubbings from them and compared patterns and shapes from the different manufacturers. How many of us have wished that we had kept the collections that we valued so highly when we were children. The foreign coins, and the wartime memorabilia, brought home by fathers and uncles, stamp collections whose value would be hard to determine today. Even our Dinky or Corgi toys are now treasures.

DUDLEY
JEROME
WHILE YOU WAIT

The war is at an end. The bunting that had decorated every street in the country is now packed away. The Victory marches are over. The music and dancing to tunes like Glen Miller's 'Chattanooga Choo-Choo', which had earned him a gold disc in 1942, have ended. You can now leave your lights on when you open the curtains. There is no fear of a visit from the air-raid warden. Gas masks are packed in their boxes and put away on top of the wardrobe in the back bedroom. The euphoria has faded. Britain's new Prime Minister, Clement Attlee, has brought the people back to earth with a bump. He has warned them of the harsh reality that there will be no immediate prosperity, but they will have to keep their ration books for a long time to come. If the children seen here shopping in Dudley Street are to have an Easter egg of any size this Easter in 1946, it will require the generosity of relatives and friends to pool their ration book coupons in order to buy it. But the sun is shining, fathers, uncles, and brothers are home, so dress to your best and go shopping for whatever may be available. Drop a gentle hint to the drivers that one day this area will belong to the pedestrian. The car is not king here.

Many of the buildings seen in our photograph still look very much the same as they did in 1946, but one has to wonder what the people of this era would have made of 'Anne Summers'! 'Joan's Fashions' are probably more their style.

It is surprising how the everyday, mundane things of the time attract the modern eye. We do not realise until we gaze back over the years how many changes have occurred, not just to the buildings on Dudley Street, but to our attitudes. It has been asked many times before, but it is worth asking again, could we park a bicycle outside a shop? Without locking it to the railings, could we expect it to be there when we returned? Just how much have we progressed? In some ways we have turned full circle, for the 'fish-bowl' gas lamps above the pavement on the left and above James Baker and Sons, would be snapped up by a television 'make-over' programme of today. It would become the focal point in a 'Ground Force' project.

Car heaters were not particularly efficient, even when they were fitted. It was more comfortable for a passenger to cover the knees with a car rug. In the summer, however the roof panel could be slid back to get the benefit of the fresh air. Spare wheels are easily accessible, but there is little boot space in even the largest vehicle. But the most comfortable vehicle of all is the coach built pram on the well-sprung chassis coming out of Woolworth's. There was even room at the bottom below the baby's feet, for those bargains which were available at 'Woolies'. A proper pram, not easy to get on and off a bus we'll grant you, but we walked to most places we wanted to go and the baby slept deeply with the movement of the snug and warm carriage. A real pram!

Two pedestrians hesitantly move onto the crossing at the top of Victoria Street in the early fifties. The crossing is marked only by studs and a traffic island, and is about where the clock, presented to the town by Beatties PLC, now stands. It has not yet earned its zebra stripes. They have not yet been invented, and neither has the traffic warden or yellow lines, so no risk here of receiving a parking ticket. Drivers were advised in the new Highway Code booklet (issued for the first time in 1954 to every provisional licence holder) where not to park and cause a hazard to other road users, but the ones at the time this photograph was taken park where they will. The Festival of Britain had started the decade with a message of hope as life slowly returned from the austerity of the war and more goods were available in the shops. The hated ration books would soon be a thing of the past. It would be possible now to buy a television, sales of which rocketed in preparation for the coronation. What a day when neighbours were invited into the homes of those lucky enough to be able to afford one to watch the mammoth event. It was the longest continuous television programme ever to be screened! We all studied the route, which was clearly mapped out in every newspaper in the land. Every map showed the position of each television camera. Commentators passed to their colleagues as the royal coach moved along the route past the various camera locations. The entire country gazed at the small purple screen, and Granny found it hard to understand that the event was actually happening at that very moment before our very eyes!

Large posters send out a pathetic cry, but there is no one to hear. Only a few ghosts drift by. There are bargains to be found at the Irish Linen Depot in Dudley Street, as well as those offered further down the road, where 'opportunities' exist in the 'exclusive sale' at Bates'. Maybe it is simply too early in the day, and those are not ghosts, but simply workers rushing to work at a speed too quick for the shutter of the camera. It was difficult to load the old box camera. The film was unrolled from a spool and loaded into the camera in the dark. Using only the sense of touch, it required the practice of a few 'dummy runs' if the light was not to invade before the cover was locked back into place. They were simple affairs requiring little technical skill to take a picture, but the subject had to be still if a clear image was to be obtained for posterity.

Mr Smith, the fishmonger, has not yet opened the shutters to reveal the catch of the day, and Mr Bywaters, the butcher, usually had a queue of loyal customers, in these days before the supermarkets came along. Shoppers waited patiently to receive individual attention. It would have been unheard of to pick up items and put them into a basket before paying for them. Supermarkets took a little getting used to! Besides, there was something pleasant about being 'sir' or 'madam' for a moment, and to be recognised. It was good to be able to exchange a few pleasantries as your waited for the weekend joint to be wrapped.

Imagine buying a suit of clothes, no extras to pay, for the sum of fifty shillings. Translated into modern cash - two pounds and fifty pence! The pound may have bought a lot more in the 1920s, but that was still excellent value for money. It just happens to be the amount of money given to a soldier when he was demobilised from the army. He went and bought his suit, which would consist of jacket, waistcoat and trousers (no extras required), from the Fifty Shilling Tailors, or from Montague Burton's, hence the expression 'the full Monty' - this term has acquired a slightly different meaning these days! This may well be a very good deal, but it cannot compete with the bargains available in the closing down sale next door. The crowds have gathered at Stewart's window. Here a suit can be obtained for twenty-five shillings. That is one pound and twenty-five pence today. A raincoat for nine shillings and six pence! (Forty-seven and a half new pence) Little wonder that the crowd has gathered here in Dudley Street.

What a chance to replace the Sunday suit and relegate it to the everyday wear. Maybe there were bargains to be had in caps and hats, for these were the days when few went out into the world bare headed. If an overcoat could be taken for twelve and six (work that one out for yourselves, please), what was the price for a shirt and extra collars? Shirts with separate collars were still very practical right into the 1950s. By then, though, collars, held by a front and back metal collar stud, could be reversed. They could be turned inside out and replaced so that a shirt would be Persil White in the afternoon.

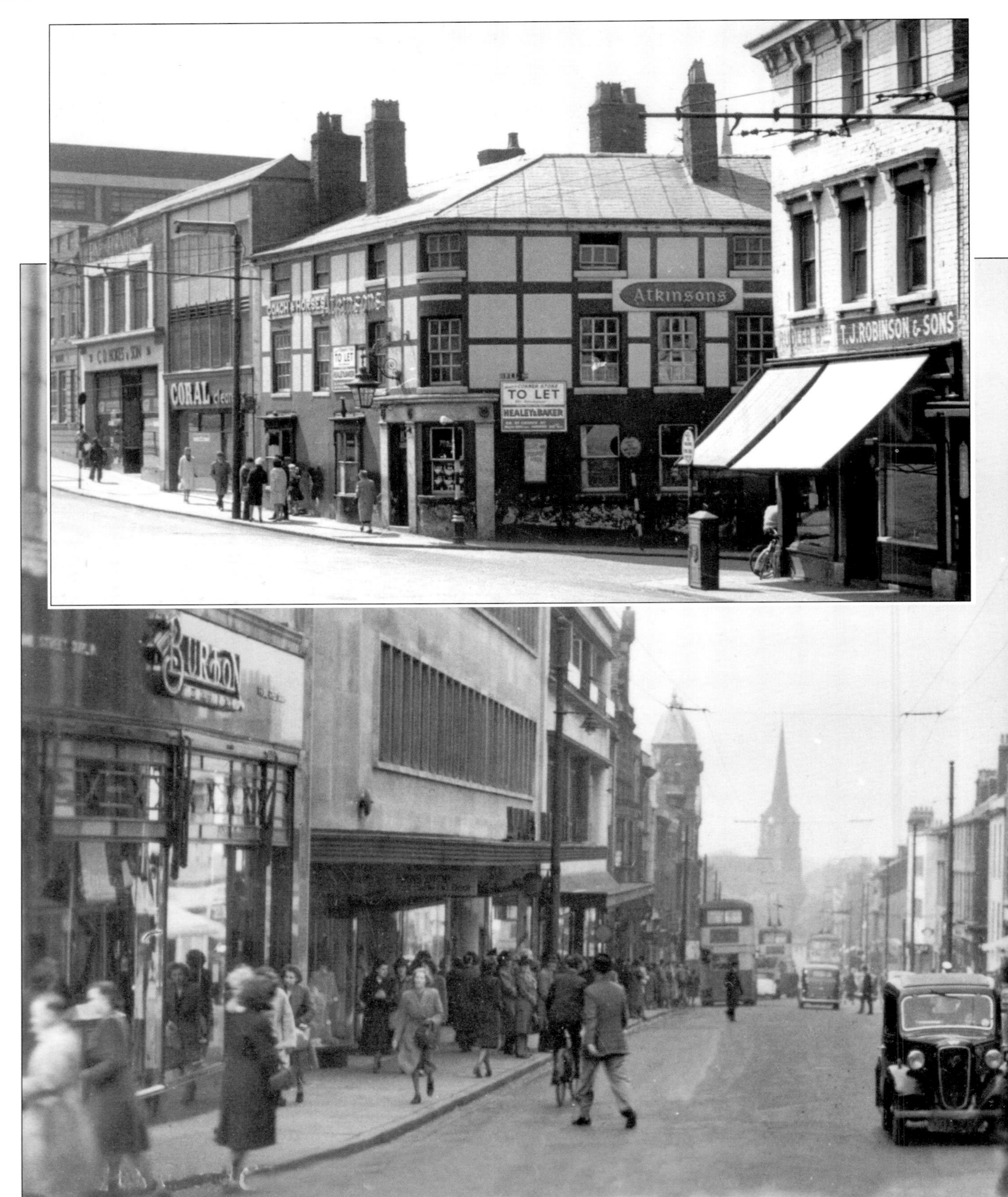
COACH & HORSES
Atkinsons
T.J.ROBINSON & SONS
CORAL
TO LET
HEALEY & BAKER
BURTON

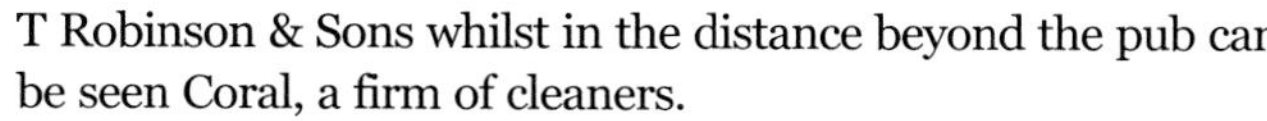

Far left: The place is Snow Hill, the date the late 1950s or early 1960s. The photographer has captured a sunny afternoon in the days before we had heard of the Beatles or the Rolling Stones let alone the Spice Girls; Elvis was still the King, even if by then his real heyday as a rock and roll singer was already past. In the centre of the picture is the Coach and Horses, a public house with a long history as a coaching inn. No doubt many readers will have enjoyed sinking a pint of Atkinsons there. At the time this picture was taken the premises were to let. Nearer to us on the right hand side of the picture is T Robinson & Sons whilst in the distance beyond the pub can be seen Coral, a firm of cleaners.

What is less obvious, until one takes a second look, are the trolley bus cables strung across the road, a reminder of the happy days of our youth when lighting a fag on the upper deck was sophisticated not banned and when a good holiday meant Butlins not two weeks in Florida.

Less obvious still, by virtue of their complete absence, are yellow lines marking the edge of the road, a reminder that once upon a time you could park your car anywhere; well you could if you were lucky enough to own one; in this picture however the only visible transport is the rear wheel of a bicycle just disappearing round the corner.

Left: These were the fifties. They began grey and dingy. The mists, through which we can just see St Mark's church, would often mix with the smoke bellowing from the chimneys of houses and factories to form a dangerous impenetrable blanket. Many people died, not only from accidents which happened in this thick 'smog', a new word coined by the newspapers to describe the toxic mix of smoke and fog, but from respiratory diseases. How many can remember having struggled home from school, from work and from shopping, finding that a wet sooty film would cover their hair and clothes? In 1956 the 'Clean Air Act' was passed, coming into action two years later.

The Austin Seven waits as shoppers cross at the top of Darlington Street. The war may have ended, but there may still be a queue at the shop. It wasn't until 1954 that people could meet in Trafalgar Square and dance and cheer as they tore up their ration books. The fifties began with the Festival of Britain setting the mood for the country. Trade and industry were becoming more buoyant, perhaps the Oxford crew could have taken a few tips from them. They sank in 1951's boat race. The weather was so bad that the umpire cancelled the race.

By the end of the fifties there would be more goods in the shops, and more in the pocket to buy them. Heralded by the first commercial television programme in 1955 the age of the consumer arrived. The first television advertisement was for SR toothpaste.

Wolverhampton's wholesale fruit and vegetable market pictured on the right in this late 1950s photograph opened in 1903 and was to remain open until 1973 when it sadly disappeared from our townscape. But these crowds are not here for fruit, they are visiting the open market seen here from within the gardens of St Peter's church. The church was originally built in 1425 though it was rebuilt in the 16th century since when little has altered, save the chancel, reconstructed in 1867.

The cameraman has kept his feet on the ground but many of those in the picture will have made the journey up the seemingly endless steps in the church tower to take in the view of the town and distant countryside. Those who made it to the top in latter days however would be rewarded with a better view. Today we can see further than was possible in those literally dark days before smokeless zones. The abundant chimney pots on the distant buildings were not simply for decoration. Though we may recall those long gone days with nostalgia not everything was better; one of the bad things was air pollution. With tens of thousands of homes burning coal for heating, not to mention factories and foundries, the air was often thick with smoke. Only the thousands of deaths experienced in a bad smog over one alarming week in London prompted the authorities to do something. Ten years after this photo was taken the air quality was massively improved.

Making a living

'Hold that pose!' calls the cameraman. 'Don't blur the image!' It is so important to record this historic moment when Wolverhampton police take delivery of this new Star ambulance. DA 2992 was bought with money raised by the Special Constabulary and presented to the Chief Constable in 1916. There was a war on you know! It was used up to 1931 when a Morris Commercial Vehicle replaced it.
Between the two World Wars the Borough Police provided emergency services. Twenty-four policemen were paid an extra two shillings (ten new pence) per week to be act as firemen when required to do so. They were also entitled to an extra pair of trousers.
The fire department in Wolverhampton, at this time, had only two Dennis engines. The police force were equipped with this Star ambulance, a Ford one-ton prison van, one Clyno Car, three AJS motorcycle combinations, and twelve bicycles. Six of the bikes were Sunbeams and the other six were Wearwells. With such resources at their disposal, what chance did the criminal have? That question might well have received a warm answer from the constable holding the end of the stretcher. He was PC 77, Jim Jones. He was the tallest constable on the force at that time and towered above the waifs and strays gathered to play the crowd in this melodramatic photograph. Fire Brigade Inspector Edwards watches admiringly as the child is carefully lifted from the ambulance outside the Royal Hospital and into the arms of the medical staff. Fireman Billy Dean whispers a word of comfort into the lad's ear. Florence Nightingale (this may not be the name of this particular nurse, but all other names are thought to be incorrect) waits on the steps.

DA 2992

Above: Although Wolverhampton received its attention from the Luftwaffe during their bombing raids, they cannot be blamed for the damage to the premises of the Warwickshire Furnishing Company in 1957. The ladder is in place and rescue services are carrying out their risky work. The wall does not seem safe. The policeman stops all traffic and people from entering the area until remedial work can be undertaken. The ambulance waits at the ready, so we assume that someone may have been injured when the wall collapsed.

Opposite the church of St Mary and St John in Snow Hill, there are still some buildings of the same architectural design in existence today. They have received extra support in the way of tie bars, but they remain intact. The end-plates, securing the front and back walls, are visible in several places. One of these buildings now houses 'The Tasty Bite'. It looks as though a bite has been taken out of the furnishing company!

The anxious crowd could not have imagined all the demolition which was to take place in the future as the ring road cut its way through. At the time this picture was taken ideas were being tabled for the road, and work would begin on the first phase in a few short years. At the bottom of the Hill many familiar landmarks, such as the Gaumont Palace Cinema, would disappear as the face of the town changed. If the people in this crowd did possess a crystal ball into which they could gaze at the future, would they have believed that the Pop Star, Cliff Richards, who would perform live at the Gaumont Palace just before it was demolished, would become Sir Cliff?

Above right: It is a sad day for many with the last Bilston, number seven's trip down the tracks. The posters, advertising 'Sunlight Soap', to clean the outside, and 'Andrew's Liver Salts' to clean the inside, would now have to travel the town on the sides of a trolley bus in the future. For the trams were now at the end of their useful lives. Originally in the hands of private companies, the trams had been horse drawn, or pulled by a steam powered 'tram engine'. With the introduction of the Wolverhampton Corporation Act of 1899, the council had the power to acquire all tramways. Having taken that step the decision was made

to convert them all to a standard three foot-six inch gauge track, and to electrify them by a system called the 'Lorain' system. This did not require overhead cables, but delivered electrical power to the tram through surface boxes placed between the tracks at twelve-foot intervals. Ski-shaped plates suspended beneath the tram collected the power. This gave Wolverhampton a unique place in the history of tramways, but there was a problem. Everyone else in the world was out of step! When the tram reached the boundary of the town there could be no link made with tracks and lines of neighbouring systems. Ingenious hybrids were constructed, which were fitted with poles so that they could use overhead cables. On their return to Wolverhampton's border they could be secured beneath a hook and the tram proceeded along the Lorain track. The Penn Fields route was converted from the Lorain system to overhead in October of 1921, and ceased service altogether in March 1927.

The Goodyear Tyre Company has been a major employer in Wolverhampton from the day of its official opening by the mayor in 1927 to the present day. In two short years they celebrated the production of the millionth tyre. By 1964 it was a staggering fifty million tyres, many of which were for the aeroplane industry, which Goodyear had produced. When the company celebrated its Silver Jubilee in 1952, eighty-six employees were awarded silver pins for twenty-five years of loyal service. Goodyear has always had a large female workforce. They were all expected to wear trousers and sleeveless blouses, in order to avoid accidents caused when loose clothing became entangled in machinery. This may seem today to be an innocent statement to make, but trousers were considered to be for men only, and 'rather risqué' and suggestive on the ladies. Many eyebrows were

raised! War work did much to change this attitude, but the land army girls achieved 'pin-up' status equal to any 'page three girl' because they wore trousers.

Not all of the years were easy, and, like many other companies in the country in 1974, a three-day week had to be introduced because of the energy crisis. The miners were in conflict with Ted Heath's Conservative government. They were operating an overtime ban, in what was described by Lord Carrington, the Minister for Energy, as, 'The most serious crisis in peacetime that any of us can recall'.

This is the tyre room in 1932. The following year Sir Malcolm Campbell drove his car 'Bluebird', at Daytona Beach in Florida, to set up a new land speed record of 272 miles per hour. In 1966 the world racing title was won on Goodyear tyres.

'Watch the birdie, ladies', calls the photographer as they pose outside Guy Motors Ltd factory at Fallings Park, Wolverhampton, during those busy war years. No point trying to take the picture inside, because all the windows were covered to comply with the black-out regulations. Conditions within the factory would have been very uncomfortable. Maybe they are smiling for the sheer relief of being out in the sunshine away from the constant electric light. These ladies willingly took on the retraining necessary, and filled the jobs traditionally done by the men. Posters cried out for the women to work in the factories, and the government were overwhelmed by the response.

Soon they would be back to the production of vehicles to fill the urgent government contract for military

vehicles. A variety of military equipment was produced, as well as the six-wheeled lorries. They made the Quad-Ant gun tractors, and even a light tank. From 1941 they also supplied civilian vehicles for approved hauliers who had been allocated a special licence from the Ministry. These were called the Vix-ant, which were based on the Vixen with many of the Guy Ant military vehicle parts were incorporated.

Sydney Slater Guy had left the Sunbeam Motor Company, where he was works manager, in 1914. He started his own company producing his own design of commercial vehicles. Almost immediately he was involved in wartime production. Peacetime vehicles included the well-known Vixen and Wolf lorries. From 1934, the famous Red Indian face smiled out from the, now much collected, badges above the radiator. They carried the motto, 'Feathers in our cap'.

Below: 'Where are we now Harry?' 'We're in Princess Street. Just passing Mitchell's. Let's make a cup of tea.' 'Can't straighten up, Harry!' 'Whose daft idea was it to paint white lines in the road anyway?'
As the number of cars on the roads increased, more and more laws were made to control their use. In 1927 white lines were first used as road dividers. Speedometers became mandatory on cars in Britain during the same year, although the 30 mph speed limit did not come into being until 1934. In 1930 it became law to have third party insurance cover, and to report certain accidents. In 1934 the driving tests were introduced for those who did not already hold a licence.
The Highway Code did not come into being until 1954. It was issued to every provisional licence holder, and to every driver when their licence was renewed. Members of the public could buy one for one penny. The book contained methods of giving hand signals. Making a circle with the right arm in order to indicate that it was the intention to turn left was always a risky manoeuvre. Waving the extended right arm up and down to show that the car was about to stop. Drum brakes were not as efficient as modern disc brakes, and 'gearing down' was an essential part of the braking process. In the fifties, syncromesh gears were a new innovation. Prior to their introduction each time the driver had to change gear, he had to 'double de-clutch'. It was a complicated action necessary to stop the gears from grinding together. It wasn't until as late as 1965 that brake lights and flashing indicators had to be fitted to all new cars.

Right: The trams had gone from Wellington Road in Bilston, but they had left behind a pleasant grass island creating a wide dual carriageway. The fine wrought iron gas lamps, copied today as attempts are made to recapture our past. On the day our shutter snapped they were receiving the necessary maintenance and clean to allow the bright white light to continue to illuminate the road.
There always seemed to be something to watch on the way to school. It was more interesting than a PE lesson, even if Miss had added the new craze of hoola-hoops to the rest of the gym equipment. Watching a man on top of a scaffold, or busy digging a hole in the road received our attention in a way that lessons never did, and you can talk. Our teacher never let you talk. It is more fun than a 'Janet and John' book. If we had Sir, instead of Miss, you could always get him off the daily singsong recitation of our 'tables' by asking him what he did to win the war. Before the war, it was thought that possible to buy the way out of depression by financing building programmes, and it was true to a certain extent. After the war the programme continued, but materials were in short supply, and many were constructed 'under licence'. Lessons were learnt about the prefabrication of parts to construct a home quickly. Many who lived in the 'prefabs' of the time liked their cosy homes and, because of their popularity, bungalows existed for a long time beyond their intended life. Other houses contained standard prefabricated units such as metal window frames. Attempts were made to give each individuality by the addition of timber to give a 'Tudor' look.

THE BILSTON GAS
LIGHT & COKE Co Ltd
PHONE 41402
GAS TO BE SURE
GRE 679

I bet that the chap who dug that hole drinks Guinness! Remember the adverts depicting a man carrying a horse across his shoulders. 'Guinness is good for you!' or so we were led to believe. Work is in full swing now for the centre development. This corner has witnessed many dramatic changes throughout the years. Perhaps 'dramatic' is the right word to use for, once upon a time, there stood, about where the photographer stood to snap this picture in 1967, the Gaumont Palace. It had been built in 1932, in the art deco style, on the site of the old Agricultural Hall. The Gaumont Palace staged many a good film and live concert. At the commencement of many an evening's show, the audience would be lulled by a medley of popular tunes played on the Cinema's Compton Organ. Hidden by the darkness the audience would hum the catchy tunes, before the cock crowed to herald British Movietone News. Prior to its' closure in 1973, Cliff Richard gave a live show in this theatre. The doors closed after a nostalgic showing of 'Singing in the Rain', on the 10th November 1973. Most of the cinemas of this period saw their end coming when the Betting and Gaming Act of 1961 allowed more than the previous limit of twenty pounds to be won in any one game. Bingo had arrived. There was Top-Rank Bingo at the Queen's Ballroom, and soon many cinemas followed.

Above: It is August 1966 and, for a short time, St Mark's church spire can be seen from here. Soon the new shopping centre would rise and blot out the view as the central area development goes ahead. The ring road had, by now almost encircled the town centre. These were exciting times. England won the world cup beating Germany by four goals to two, but even a girl who hates football knows that! 'They think it's all over, it is now', became one of the most quoted commentary phrases ever made.

London was a 'swinging' place to be according to chic magazines. Flower power was imported from America and Carnaby Street became the boutique centre of the fashion world. Mary Quant was a leader of the style from her Bazaar in the King's Road. The hem of the mini-skirt rose almost as high as the eyebrows of the older generation. Girls bought make-up, even if they had to rub it off on the last bus home, before mum saw it. What would the neighbours think? Parents were still reeling from the shock of the Beatles being awarded MBEs in the previous year. They were 'the pop group with the funny hair-cuts', who shot to fame with songs like 'Please Please Me'.

These were the days when the morals of Britain were on trial. Penguin Books had published the unexpurgated edition of DH Lawrence's book, 'Lady Chatterley's Lover'. They were taken to court for the law to decide whether it was art or pornography. Until then, only students of literature and other intellectuals had heard of the book. Now it would become a best seller the moment it was judged to be Art.

Chaps and taps

At the start of the new millennium the Wolverhampton site of American Standard Plumbing (UK) Ltd, perhaps locally more familiar as Armitage Shanks, was situated at the Tap Works in Showell Road in Bushbury. The location is north of Wolverhampton city centre on the edge of a residential/industrial area on a site which has been in use since the early 1920s. Over the decades thousands of Wolverhampton's world famed engineers have worked there.

THE AUTOCAR. ADVERTIS_MENTS. JUNE 23RD, 1900. 7

Star Motor Car

Design A.

Price from 160 Guineas
WITH
Clipper Tyres.
3½ h.p.

WRITE FOR OUR ILLUSTRATED LIST AND TESTIMONIALS.

Why is the Star Motor the best of its class?

BECAUSE—You have not to push up hills. See report on Hill-climbing Contest—
Taddington Hill at the rate of nine miles per hour, Birkhill eight miles per hour.
BECAUSE—It is a Gentleman's Carriage, not a seat on four wheels.
BECAUSE—Intending purchasers can always test a car on country roads and up
hills of one in ten gradient—not on London asphalt.
BECAUSE—It is exceptionally silent when travelling—not like a reaping machine
at work.
BECAUSE—It is all made at our Works, Wolverhampton. The longer it is used
the better it becomes.
BECAUSE—It is simplicity itself and can be manipulated by anyone.
BECAUSE—It is free from complicated machinery.
BECAUSE—The speed of Motor is 700 revolutions per minute—not 2,000, tearing
itself to bits.
BECAUSE—It is kept cool by water, not air, this is the most effectual and
reliable method.
BECAUSE—All competitors have to acknowledge its superiority as a hill-climber,
and it is only 3½ h.p.
BECAUSE—It is the most economical Car yet produced.
BECAUSE—F. S. Edge, one of our greatest authorities on Motoring, states the
Star to be the best Car of its class yet produced. See "Wheeling," March 28th,
1900.

STAR MOTOR CO., Stewart St., Wolverhampton

Once a very rural area the first manufacturing industry in Bushbury did not arrive in the parish until 1890 when the Electric Construction Corporation built its workshops in the gardens of Gorsebrook House on the corner of Stafford Road and the old drive to Showell Manor. Another small industry arrived at the end of the 19th century, brick-making, with brickyards on the site of what would much later become Bushbury school and another in the Jones Road and South Street area.

The increasing attractiveness of the area to industry was in part due to the railway. The first railway through the parish was the Grand Junction line from Birmingham to Warrington which entered the parish near Showell Manor. Bushbury Station was opened in 1852. Continuing developments of the railway system meant more families came to settle in the parish mainly around Bushbury Lane and Shaw Road, where new houses were built in the 1870s and 80s, followed by Showell Road in the 1890s, which would, 30 years later, see the appearance of a new motor car factory.

Above: *Advertising the Star Motor Car, in 1900.* ***Below:*** *Star Cars on exhibition at the Paris Motor Show during December 1905.*

In 1922 a 22 acre site in Showell Road was bought by the Star Motor Company, a Wolverhampton firm, which already produced motor vehicle bodies, most notably the Star Car - (up to the end of the 20th century some A-Z maps were still showing the site as 'Motor Works').

The first Star car, based on the Benz, had come out of the company's Stewart Street premises in 1899; it had a 3.5 horsepower water cooled engine and cost 160 guineas; the following year a twin cylinder car became available. Sales were good and in 1905 a cheaper car was introduced, the Starling which sold for £110. That same year Star introduced commercial vehicles to its product range.

The first six cylinder Star came out during 1907 and by 1911 Star was amongst the six largest car makers in the country.

Soon after the end of the first world war in 1918 the Star Motor Company had a full range of cars on the market and in 1921 introduced a 11.9 hp light car. Larger manufacturing premises were needed and the company acquired the Showell Road site where it built the original factory covering six acres. A 3 litre car was brought out in 1924, the overhead valve version being a notably splendid tourer.

Five models were listed for 1927, but all was not well and during 1928 the company was taken over by Sidney Guy's car company Guy Motors which continued to make Star cars alongside the Guy 18 horse power Comet and the Guy Planet until 1932.

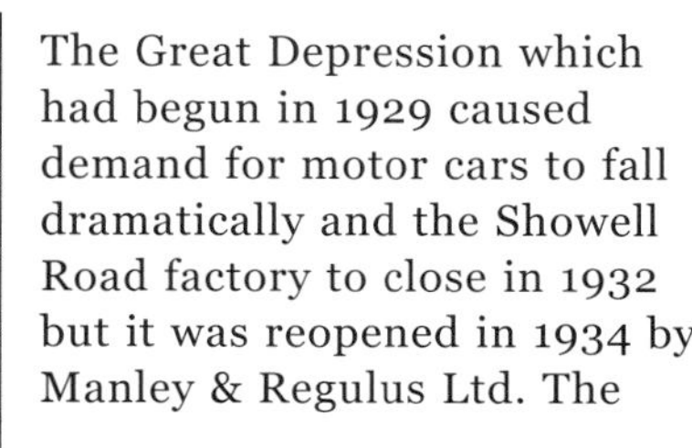

The Great Depression which had begun in 1929 caused demand for motor cars to fall dramatically and the Showell Road factory to close in 1932 but it was reopened in 1934 by Manley & Regulus Ltd. The

***Top:** Manley & Regulas fittings used on Wolverhamptons' fire-fighting float during World War II. **Left:** The fire brigade in action in March 1939, using Manley & Regulas hoses.*

new arrival had been created in 1919 by the amalgamation of two other firms WH Manley & Co. Ltd and the Regulus Metal and Plumbing Co. Ltd. The partnership of WH Manley and PJ Jemmet heating and plumbing contractors which began in 1884 would be a story of outstanding achievements in engineering.

During the Great War of 1914-18 the partnership had concentrated mainly on the design, manufacture and installation of acid resisting valves for use in munitions factories producing TNT and, as considerable quantities of such valves were required, the Regulus Metal Company was established to handle that side of the business. Following the end of the war the demand for acid resisting valves not unexpectedly became very small and it was decided to amalgamate the manufacturing capabilities of what was then WH Manley & Co. and the Regulus Metal Company to develop the production of plumbers' fittings.

As the new company of Manley & Regulus Ltd began to expand it was found that its premises in the centre of Wolverhampton was inadequate and the move to the former Guy's factory on Showell Road was made in 1934.

Manley & Regulus manufactured water fittings at Showell Road beginning a connection with that trade which would continued for generations. A press shop was established increasing the range of taps manufactured and which also enabled machined parts to be supplied to the trade. The company produced a range of water fittings and associated items based on brass casting. The move enabled the company to meet an increasing demand for its brass pressings; now it was decided to utilise available space for the installation of a modern hot brass pressing plant using crank and screw friction presses.

The site was shared with a building company, McKiend Smith, and a firm of plumbers, Wiseman Brothers, who occupied 20 per cent of the site. During the mid 1930s the remainder of the 22 acre site was turned over to housing development with the newly erected dwellings being rented to company employees. Many employees put their name on 'the list' as soon as they had completed the qualifying time of six months employment.

Top: *Turning out shell components for the war effort during WWII.* ***Above right and right:*** *Before and after pictures of the reconstruction of the Stamping Shop at Showell Road, 1963-1965.*

building and plumbing companies were relocated though the housing estate became the property of Douglas C Jemmett the former Managing Director of Manley & Regulus and the Jemmett family. The houses were subsequently offered for sale to sitting tenants.

For some the change in ownership meant a major change in their working lives, for others it was business as usual. Employment levels were high everywhere as were expectations of what the future would hold. The 1960s were optimistic times even if that optimism could sometimes be tempered with tragedy, as for example in 1965 when an explosion in the boiler house killed one man and severely burned another.

During the second world war the factory turned to producing bomb fuses and 'tank vent valves', devices mainly used on Wellington bombers to cut fuel to engines in the case of fire.

If making war material did not make the point the close proximity of the factory to railway would bring the war quickly to the attention of workers at the factory. In 1940 trainloads of exhausted troops evacuated from Dunkirk found themselves stuck in carriages nearby whilst engines were changed. People from the factory and houses in the surrounding area brought jugs of tea and sandwiches for the men until the trains moved on north once more.

After the war's end in 1945 the factory produced water fittings and radiator valves. By then the firm was being run by the Managing Director Douglas Jemmett and his brother Derek Jemmett the Sales Director; both were active members of Wolverhampton Aero Club and in the 1950s took part in the Kings Cup air races.

In 1963 the Delta group of companies bought the company and the site; the building was reroofed and refloored as well as being extended at the rear where an office block and reception were added. In 1965 Delta Water Fittings was established with the amalgamation under one roof of Manley & Regulus, EP Jenks, Henry Bissiker, Sperryn & Co., J Webb and Conex Sanbra. At that time the associated

During the mid 1970s the company name was changed to Deltaflow Limited and gravity die-casting replaced stamping. The building which would later become the Toolroom was built during this period as a canteen and training centre.

In 1985 the Delta Group sold the site to Blue Circle Industries and became part of the Armitage Shanks group of companies and began trading under that name. Four years later a £1.1 million investment was made to upgrade the foundry.

Blue Circle Industries announced in February 1999 that it had completed the sale of its bathroom division to American Standard Companies Inc., the largest bathroom company in the world and the Showell Road site became part of the Ideal Standard Group. At the beginning of the new millennium the site would find itself trading as American Standard Plumbing (UK) Ltd whilst keeping the brand names of Armitage Shanks and Ideal Standard.

Top left: *Derek Jemmett, 2nd right, when he took part in the King' Cup air race, June 1950.* ***Above left:*** *Delta taps on the finishing line, circa 1965.* ***Below:*** *Douglas Jemmett is pictured 3rd from right with fellow members of Woverhampton Aero Club, 1963.*

A growing fern

When fire gutted the premises of Fern Plastic Products Ltd in Cross Street North in March 1973 it could have been the end of one of Wolverhampton's most promising young companies. Fortunately the workforce pulled together and, although having to work under a tarpaulin roof, were soon back into production.

Fern Plastic Products Ltd, today based in Macrome Road, began life in 1959 as the Fern Engineering Company. It's founders were Gilbert Joseph Guest (known as Joe) who, after starting out as a self employed tool maker, was later joined by his brother in law Ernest Peter Walker (known as Peter) a commercial traveller.

The business began as toolmakers making die casting and mould tools and started out in tiny rented premises in Fern Road off Lea Road in Penn. Joe looked after production whilst Peter looked after sales and deliveries to customers. Joe's wife Mary carried out the book keeping.

In 1962 the firm changed its name to Fern Plastic Products and moved to a factory in Temple Street, the name change reflecting a change of emphasis in the firm's products.

The company moved to its ill-fated Cross Street North premises off Cannock Road in 1967 into what was then a brand new factory. Despite rebuilding after the fire the premises soon became too small for the growing business and a move was made to Macrome Road in 1979 where an 11,500 sq. ft. factory was built, which has since expanded to 46,000 sq. ft.

Soon after the move, the company felt the impact of the 1980 recession, which meant that a number of employees were made redundant and others reduced to a three day working week. Fortunately, the business survived

A second generation now manages the business Alan Geoffrey Warrington, the son-in-law of Joe Guest, and John Charles Walker the youngest son of Peter Walker. Sadly Joe Guest died in 1986.

Today Fern's plastic injection mouldings are used by many household names such as Electrolux, Sanyo, Yale Locks and Chubb. The company employs more than 100 people, operates 24 hours a day and produces over 40 million components annually for customers throughout the British Isles and Europe: an achievement all the more remarkable for having such modest beginnings.

Above: *Founders, Peter Walker (left) and Joe Guest.*
Below: *The company's Cross Street North premises.*

A jewel of a business

Diamonds are a girl's best friend. And today any girl looking for a diamond is more than likely to look in the window of Millers Jewellers in Wolverhampton's Cleveland Street if she wants to find a diamond destined for her.

Millers Jewellers was founded in 1866, the same year that the first diamond was discovered in South Africa. The founder was William Hugh Miller a watchmaker and jeweller whose premises were then at 97 Sutton Street in Sheffield. Those first premises were demolished in the 1880s and for the next 20 years the business was run from Lichfield in the shadow of the cathedral to which Millers were contracted as official clock keepers.

In 1900 the Millers moved to Wolverhampton and the cobbled streets of Snowhill where the Millers took a large double fronted shop and workshop from where the firm traded under the name of the 'Diamond House'. Projecting from the Diamond House was an enormous double-sided clock (known as the bus driver's timepiece) beneath which many a romantic assignation took place. Often in the depths of winter the founder's grandson Alfred Miller could be seen stretching out from an upper window with a long handled broom brushing snow from the minute hands of the clock which was preventing the hands from getting past quarter to the hour.

The company moved to the Central Arcade in 1964 due to compulsory purchase and finally, following another compulsory purchase, in 1968, to its present address in the Wulfrun shopping precinct

Six generations of the Miller family would eventually be involved in running the firm. Today the family members involved in the business are the founder's great, great, great granddaughter Elizabeth Miller and her husband David Nicholls and son Richard Nicholls, himself the great, great, great, great grandson of William Miller.

Today's Millers still have clients whose families bought from the firm a century ago; their continuing pride and interest in their craft is amply attested to by the Millers freely providing guest speakers to deliver up to 60 talks every year on all aspects of the history of the jewellery trade, with bookings being taken up to three years in advance.

Top left: *A familiar sight to the people of Wolverhampton, the Millers double sided clock.*
Left: *Pictured in 1967 when three generations of the Miller family worked in the shop, from left to right Mrs Marjorie Miller, Mr William Hugh Miller (great, great grandson of the founder), Mrs Anne Miller, Mr Alfred William Miller, (great grandson of the founder), and Miss Elizabeth Miller (great, great, great granddaughter of the founder).* ***Below left:*** *The company's Wulfrun shopping precinct premises.*
Below right: *Richard Nicholls, (great, great, great, great-grandson of the founder), taken at his graduation, now a Director with the company.*

On the move

One of Wolverhampton's best known local removal firms is that of George Kertland & Son who for over three quarters of the 20th century would help thousands of ordinary Wolverhampton people move home, in addition celebrities such as the late football hero Billy Wright and TV celebrity Dale Winton.

The business was established in 1925 by George Kertland with the help of his father John Wilson Kertland.

The small business was then engaged in general haulage and removals. The firm was based in Bright Street where the business remained for ten years before moving to Molineux Street (on a site since demolished and now under Wolves' new stand) where it would stay for another 25 years before finally relocating to its present base in Newhampton Road West.

Over the decades the firm would suffer from the many problems posed by such events as the great depression of the 1930s, the war years of 1939-45 and the fuel crisis of the 1970s, yet despite those difficulties the business would eventually grow and prosper.

But before becoming the firm it is today the business had many hurdles to conquer. Not least those posed by the Depression. In 1925 when the firm was founded the country was still enjoying an economic boom, a legacy of the Great War which had ended in 1918. The 'roaring twenties' were a time of plenty with a good deal of confidence in the future and a time of relatively high employment. Many marriages had been put off until the end of the war with the consequence that young and growing families were now constantly on the move to larger houses providing plenty of business for removal firms.

No wonder that in that climate George Kertland had the confidence to invest his hard saved money in a motor van. Business was booming and he naturally assumed it would continue when in 1929 he bought his

Top left: *Founder George Kertland.* ***Above right:*** *The company's first van bought in 1925.* ***Right:*** *A George Kertland removal van from 1929.*

second van for £350. Little could he or anyone else have predicted just what a dreadful year 1929 would turn out to be. The Wall Street Crash of 1929 which followed the irrational frenzy of investment which had raised share prices to absurdly high levels led to world-wide recession.

The economic downward spiral which engulfed the USA soon found its way to the rest of the world, to Britain and more particularly to Wolverhampton where thousands soon found themselves out of work and on the dole.

With work hard to come by fewer people had the means to move house and the Kertlands found themselves in as much trouble as everyone else. Any work was welcome and at cut price rates too: a house move to Birmingham could be got for as little as £3 or £4. hardly yachts and champagne money!

Things could only get better but it would take some time; more than 15 years in fact with a war in between times. During the second world war George was called up leaving brother Ron to continue to run the business helped by George's wife Grace who had to struggle with the problems posed by petrol rationing, a difficulty which would extend far beyond the war's end in 1945.

Things did however eventually improve. George returned from the war, petrol rationing ended and the firm was able to benefit from the sustained economic growth which followed.

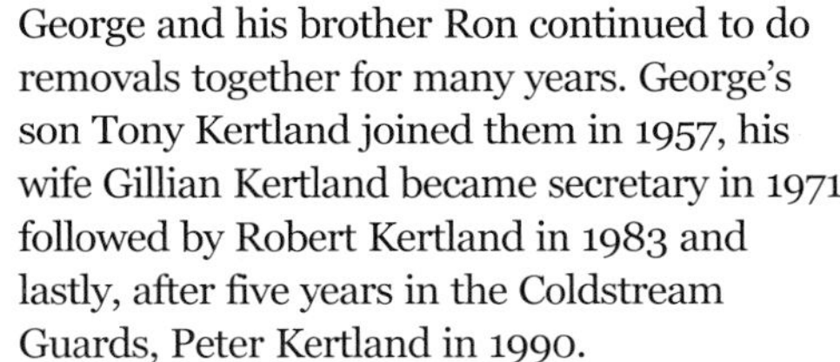

George and his brother Ron continued to do removals together for many years. George's son Tony Kertland joined them in 1957, his wife Gillian Kertland became secretary in 1971, followed by Robert Kertland in 1983 and lastly, after five years in the Coldstream Guards, Peter Kertland in 1990.

A celebration in the year 2000 of 75 years of business was held at the Punch Bowl in Bridgnorth attended by 200 people made up of family, friends and work colleagues

Over the years many changes have been seen at the firm and today the business operates a fleet of vehicles ranging from 3 1/2 ton to 16 ton gross which ensures that the business is large enough to cope with anything though still small enough to care about everything.

Offering a nationwide service and containerised storage, and with the next generation ready to continue the business, this is one firm which looks set to be on the move for many more years to come.

Top left: *Manoeuvring an organ down the steps of the Theatre in Bridgnorth.*
Left: *Tony, Gillian, Robert and Peter at their Newhampton Road West premises.*

Oranges and Lemons

The Wholesale Market at Hickman Avenue, East Park was opened by Wolverhampton Council in 1973 to meet the demand for a modern distribution centre. The market's previous location in St Peter's Square had been in use since 1902 and was no longer able to cope with the increasing volume of trade or provide convenient access to large goods vehicles. In fact the market's origins can be traced back to 1875 and the vegetable market in Cheapside, North Street and St Peter's Walk.

Occupying stands 12, 13 and 14 one of the businesses in the new market which can trace its own beginnings at least as far back as 1902 is that of H Goodall Ltd which then, as now, took great pride in supplying top quality salads, fruit, vegetables and 'exotics.

The firm was founded in 1902 by Harry Goodall as a fruit and vegetable importers, Harry was helped by his wife and in those days they moved their wares by train, horse and cart and barrow in wicker baskets and orange boxes - a far cry from today's fork lift trucks, wooden pallets, trolleys, vans and lorries.

In 1902 fruit and vegetables would be delivered to the market very early in the morning arriving from the railway station on horse drawn carts to be off loaded in the dim gas light. In winter the horse's breath steaming in the cold air would remind the stallholders of just how cold they were, though the effort of unloading sacks of potatoes from the back of carts would be enough to warm even the coldest blood - and perhaps prompt them to spare a thought for the poor horses and to offer them a carrot for their efforts.

Goods would arrive in Wolverhampton not just from farms in the Midlands but from all over the world. The produce came from what was then still the British Empire arriving in steam ships from far flung and far sunnier climes bringing oranges, limes and bananas to customers hungry for fruits which only a few generations earlier would have been virtually unknown.

And for some years they became almost unknown again. In the years 1940 to 1945 the U-boats of the

Below: *Harry Goodall's fruit and vegetable stall at the Wholesale Market, St Peter's Square, 1915.*

German navy sank so much British merchant shipping that few of the ships which remained could be spared to carry foreign fruit to Britain's shores. Goodalls like every other fruit and vegetable wholesalers soon find itself largely limited to selling what it could get from domestic producers.

But such hardship would not last forever. Older readers will recall the astonishment with which some children greeted the arrival of the very first bananas at the war's end. Sure they'd heard of bananas, even seen pictures of them, but what did you do with them, did you peel them or eat them skin and all? Happily today such critical questions no longer face our youngsters.

But war or peace being a fruit wholesaler has always involved considerable hard work and the ability to get up early in the morning, and in the past the work must have been utterly exhausting. Even today the wholesale market is open to customers from 5 am every Tuesday, Thursday, Friday and Saturday and from 6 am on Mondays and Wednesdays with deliveries being made to the market throughout the night - selling fruit and veg is certainly no job for anyone who likes to sleep in!

In 1961 Phil Sayce started work for Goodalls and was made a director in 1975, at around that time Mrs Goodall died and Shorrocks fruit wholesalers took over the business. Phil Sayce was, however, eventually able to acquire the firm and would be helped to run the business by his brother Chris until the latter's retirement.

Aaron Sayce joined the firm in 1988 and is now a director alongside Dave Hough who began working for the business in 1980.

Today Goodall's supplies to retail and secondary wholesalers and caterers throughout the region; the firm's service includes making free deliveries in their distinctive lorries within a 30 mile radius of Wolverhampton on six days a week, with Goodall's fruit and vegetables appearing in market stalls, shops and the catering trade across the whole of the Midlands.

Above left: *Busy at work in the early days.* ***Above right:*** *One of the firm's fleet of lorries.* ***Left:*** *The 2001 sales team, from left to right, Andy, Aaron, Phil and Dave.*

The complete shopping experience

The experience of shopping in Wolverhampton has come a long way since the first market stalls gave way to permanent shops. Those first shops were almost all owned by their proprietors. Later would come the national chains which so dominate all our high streets and our memories Woolworth's, Marks and Spencer's and of course Burtons the fifty shilling tailors.

But times and fashions change. Old buildings give way to new, brick replaces stone and that in turn gave way to concrete. And streets which became clogged with traffic would give way to pedestrian precincts.

Long before the expression 'retail therapy' was coined to describe the happy feeling we sometimes get from going shopping the idea of a covered shopping centre had already born fruit; the Victorians gave Britain hundreds of shopping arcades and dozens of fine covered markets, many of which have now sadly been demolished in the name of progress. The 1960s however saw the 20th century's answer to that Victorian challenge, the rise of the modern 'shopping centre'. But by the end of the century some of those novelties of the sixties were in urgent need of refurbishment and rebuilding.

In Wolverhampton first there was a rumour, and people's hopes began to rise; then it was official, and the news gladdened the hearts of local shoppers: the Wulfrun shopping centre was to be given a facelift, and work was scheduled to start in late August 1998.

As many of those shoppers would recall the Wulfrun Centre had been built between 1966 and 1969, in two phases. Each phase was greeted with tremendous enthusiasm; situated off Dudley Street and extremely convenient for the bus station, the new Centre introduced an increasing number of the big-name chain stores to Wolverhampton, and brought the latest in 60s

Above: *The Wulfrun Centre, 1968.* ***Below:*** *The Centre pictured in December 1970.*

and 70s fashion, entertainment and novelty goods within reach. Equally its paved areas with seating and landscaping features made it a pleasant place to spend time, strolling up and down the arcades, stopping for a snack and a chat with friends, and returning for another leisurely spell of window-shopping before making the final decision on the day's purchases. The Centre's popularity lasted for many years, but inevitably it began to show its age. As the 80s turned into the 90s and new concepts in shopping centre design were developed, the Wulfrun Centre's open walkways and concrete facades began to look dated. Because of its prime location, the Centre had managed to trade successfully, but it was a long time since it had excited shoppers; this, however, was about to change.

This page: *Two views of the exterior of the Wulfrun Centre in 1970.*

In August 1998 work began on a 13-month project to revitalise the Wulfrun Centre.

The refurbishment scheme was planned by London and Cambridge Properties, who purchased the centre in 1994. In drawing up the plans, LCP worked closely with the council and used the services of international architects Chapman Taylor Partners. The Centre remained open throughout the construction period, and much of the work was carried out at night, in order to minimise disruption for both shoppers and traders. LCP invested £8m in the scheme, and much careful planning was done to ensure that, by the millennium, 'visitors to the Wulfrun Centre had a better, safer and more attractive shopping environment.'

The new development made available an extra 3,000 square feet of retail space, and even before work commenced the plans had aroused a tremendous amount of interest amongst potential new traders; the first store to snap up a spot was the toy shop chain The Entertainer, which was immensely impressed with LCP's proposals, and many other major retailers followed suit.

In addition the Metro Line, linking the heart of Wolverhampton to Birmingham was completed in 1999. The terminus station in Wolverhampton is situated on the Centre's doorstep and is helping to bring a whole new generation of shoppers to the Wulfrun Centre.

And the appearance of the Wulfrun Centre has been totally transformed. The open-air malls are covered with glazed rooflights making the Centre a cheerful, comfortable and welcoming place no matter what the weather. Outside are new entrance canopies, as well as the imposing new entrance facing Dudley Street. The Bell Street end was completely altered, the narrow curved mall realigned to form a focal point, and the central circus area and Wulfrun Square have become another focal point featuring a new mall café. New seating areas have been provided, as well as new public toilets incorporating facilities for the disabled and for mother and baby. In short, the new Wulfrun Centre has everything one could wish for, combining shopping and entertainment under one glass roof with easy access to both public transport and ample car parking.

It was an ambitious scheme, but one which Wolverhampton, an established market town with an estimated shopping population of 500,000, was ready for. When the new Wulfrun Centre was completed in time for the next century shopping in Wolverhampton once again became an exciting and stimulating experience, as it was when the Wulfrun Centre was first opened in the 60s. Wolverhampton entered the new millennium as a strong, thriving shopping and entertainment centre, and the new Wulfrun Centre would be at its very heart. Following its reopening in 1999 the Wulfrun Centre would welcome many new traders such as TK Maxx, Mac's Cosmetics, Premier Leathers, Tantastic, Book Sale, Kids Kamp and Hillary's Blinds alongside the other now well established businesses. And the Wulfrun Centre would aim to make shopping accessible to everyone including the less able and young families. With that in mind the centre would became home to Wolverhampton's Shopmobility facility providing wheelchairs and scooters to disabled shoppers as well as a clean and modern baby changing suite.

From Morrelli's Cappuccino giving a continental feel to the oriental East West Chinese food store the Wulfrun Centre would have something for everyone. The shoppers from long ago might have some difficulty recognising the modern town but today's shoppers will certainly have no difficulty recognising the Wulfrun Centre as the place to shop in the 21st century.

Above: *The newly refurbished New Wulfrun Square.*
Below: *The modern entrance to the Wulfrun Centre, pictured in 2001.*

Live wires of quality

The immediate postwar years were hardly the best of times to launch a new business, although there was work to be done, materials were in short supply in our war ravaged nation. They were indeed austere days but, with a sense of purpose and a determination to succeed, it was possible to achieve positive results. Being imbued with such an attitude brought the corresponding rewards for JT Jarvis & Son Limited, a family firm founded by John T Jarvis, known as Jack, and his son, Jim T Jarvis.

The business, then called Jarvis Electricians, was initially based at 18 Rosemary Avenue, a private house on the Goldthorn Park Estate. It did not take long for the Jarvis reputation for quality workmanship to spread and, as business increased, it soon became necessary to move to larger premises in Bell Street. So well was the company doing that it even outgrew this site and in 1954 moved on again, this time to 22 Cleveland Street, when the present name of the firm was adopted.

At this time a medium sized contracting department was soon established and, as the town centre was improved, the retail department developed with a large range of lighting fittings and appliances being stocked. It was a true family concern as Jack's wife, Lilian, and Jim's wife, Olive, were also involved in the business. Jack, who had been working part time, retired from his job as a maintenance engineer with Mander Brothers in 1957 and took over the management of the shop showrooms and repair department until his death in 1970.

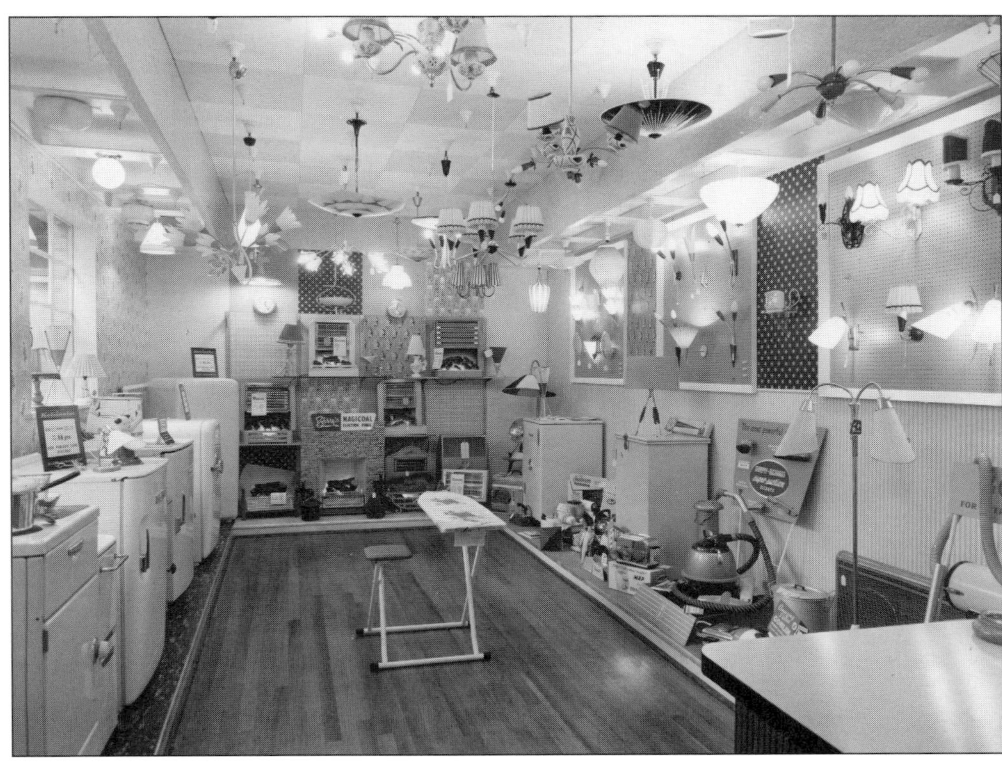

Jim is now the managing director and was joined by his son, another John T Jarvis, in the mid 1970s, making it three generations of involvement in a company that serves both the general public as well as commercial premises. Always faithful to the ethic of pride in its work, customer satisfaction in the quality of work carried out by this firm of electrical contractors remains high in their minds, knowing they have had value for their money.

Above: *Jim and John Jarvis.* ***Left:*** *An interior view of the showroom in the 1950s.*

Latin love and romance

When McLean's demolished an old garage on School Street and built its office block and various shops little did it know that it was later to share in a business development and love story that would touch the hardest of hearts.

That part of the history of the Pepito restaurant was yet to be written when Joe Conti, an Italian from Padova, opened his doors to diners for the first time in 1964. He drew upon his previous experience in catering as he built up a clientele that was looking for more exotic alternatives to the traditional fare served up in British restaurants.

In the swinging 60s people were in the mood for change as they became more adventurous and experimented with food other than the basic meat and two veg or that good old standby of fish and chips. Oriental eating places, French bistros, Greek and Italian restaurants all offered a rich variety for this new breed of discerning diner.

Package holidays abroad had opened the eyes of many, as well as their mouths, to the delights of rich sauces, subtle flavours and blended spices. It was a far cry from stodgy Yorkshire pud and apple crumble as a culinary revolution came to the streets of Britain in general and, in particular, to those where there was a healthy multicultural mix.

It was within this climate that Pepito prospered as Joe Conti's cuisine received praise and recommendation that spread the length and breadth of Wolverhampton. It became a favourite of couples looking for a quiet evening together in a romantic setting, whilst enjoying good food.

But our love story does not focus on any of Mr Conti's customers from the 1960s, nor does it even begin in the Black Country, but in Milan, the capital city of Italian Lombardy. William Catellani had left his home town of Reggio and come to work in Milan, running a restaurant in the city.

William owed the choice of his Christian name to the fact that his parents used to work for a member of the English nobility and thought it suited their son.

One happy day in 1958 a student of foreign languages chanced to enter William's restaurant whilst taking a break from her lessons. The 18 year old Emilia took one look at the owner's handsome face and immediately fell under the spell of his charismatic manner. If ever she doubted such a thing as love at first sight, then those doubts went out of the window the moment he turned towards her and smiled that melting smile of his. William, too, felt as if fate had brought them together and they soon became inseparable. But, true love does not run smooth, even in Italy. Emilia's parents felt that she was too young to commit herself to marriage. As she was under 21 she could not marry without their consent and so they packed her off to England to further her language studies and to forget all about William.

Resourceful as ever, William followed Emilia to England and used the opportunity to elope

***Above:** William and Emilia Catellani.*

to Gretna Green, where they became husband and wife. As he could have been arrested for flouting Italian law, Emilia and William decided to stay on in England.

Times were tough for a young couple, but William was determined to support his bride as she continued her studies and he got a job as a butler in London.

As committed Catholics the couple wanted to solemnise their marriage in church and, after negotiations with bishops in London and Milan, they were married at the Brompton Oratory.

The 18 year old Emilia took one look at the owner's handsome face and immediately fell under the spell of his charismatic manner.

They moved back to Italy for some years, where Emilia gave birth to Vittorio and Carla, but relationships with relatives were still strained and the family returned to England in 1971. William became the chef at the Pepito restaurant and the Catellanis bought the business from Joe Conti in 1974. With a lot of hard work and effort they built up the business to such an extent that by 1984 they were able to expand by taking over adjoining premises.

Sadly, William died in 1991, but Emilia knows that he is in heaven, watching over her and the children who help their mother in the business that has built up a loyal staff and regular customer base, some of whom come from the most distinguished branches of society to enjoy the friendly atmosphere and fine cuisine served here. A doctor once told Emilia that she was built to last forever. She feels that it must be because her heart was strengthened by loving William.

Below: *William and Emilia's son Vittorio outside Pepito.*

Learning is for life

When the Labour leader, Tony Blair, swept into power in 1997 it was partly on the election ticket of his slogan, 'Education, education, education'. This was hardly news to anyone involved with Newbridge Preparatory School, for they had been supplying top quality opportunities for their pupils since before the second world war. This independent day school for girls, aged from 3 to 11 years, has always set high standards for itself in promoting literacy and numeracy as major vehicles of curricular communication. But, the school is not a crammer, churning out automatons who can read effortlessly, but without enjoyment, or compute without the wherewithal to know when or how to apply their skills.

Newbridge offers a rich and wide curriculum that ranges across all aspects from design technology to French and includes a commitment to extra curricular activities, such as music, sport and residential visits, ensuring that each girl has ample opportunity to develop her special interests as well as her all round talents. Whether it be winning prizes at the Dudley festival, singing at the Birmingham Symphony Hall or winning swimming and gymnastic championships the girls at Newbridge exhibit their prowess to a wide audience.

Above: *Children pictured at Newbridge Preparatory School in 1945.*
Right: *Newbridge Preparatory School.*
Below: *Staff and pupils pictured in 1946.*

The school was founded in September 1937 as the Homelands PNEU (Parents' National Education Union) School by Robert Milnes-Walker, an eminent local surgeon. There were just four pupils on the register that first day, including Ruth, the founder's daughter, and the headmistress, Miss Audrey Smith, was also the full complement of staff! She left in 1940, by which time there were three teachers on the staff, all of whom resided at the school.

However, the most exciting development of recent years took place in the early 1990s when a purpose built nursery for three and four year olds opened. This self contained unit, attractively sited at the bottom of the garden, lets the children feel as though they are part of the larger school without compromising their own identity. The unit has three staff, attending to the children's welfare and educational needs. In 1994, as pupil numbers increased and the advances and changes within the curriculum required addressing, the directors launched their project 'Building for the future', whereby older parts of the building would be replaced with new facilities. An appeal raised £75,000, enabling a new art and design technology room, with classroom above, to be opened. In 1996 a new music facility, ICT room, PE changing quarters and a kitchen completed the redevelopment.

Pupil numbers had grown quickly in those early days, necessitating a move to larger premises, firstly to a cottage at 15 Park Road West and then to the bigger house next door. When the founder was appointed to the post of Professor of Surgery in Bristol he decided to sell the school, suggesting that the parents form their own company in order to purchase and administrate it.

In 1946 the school became an incorporated company, the Wolverhampton PNEU School Ltd. Mr JB Brockbank was the chairman of the board of directors, whilst Mr HW Inglis acted as company secretary. Since then there have been a number of notable chairmen, down to the current incumbent, Mr P Webb. On 12 April 1949 'The Laurels' was purchased and the school moved to 51 Newbridge Crescent, where it remains today.

In 1982 the directors decided to change from membership of the PNEU to the larger, nationally recognised IAPS (Incorporated Association of Preparatory Schools).

Newbridge is a school that has a strong sense of community amongst its 150 children and staff members. Many girls are from the second generation of their families to attend the school, which is a testimonial to the high regard in which Newbridge is held by past pupils. They recall the excellent grounding they received here and feel it is only just to ensure that their daughters receive the same privileges of learning in an environment that will equip them for both future education and life itself.

The school uniform was updated at the start of this century when out went the brown and gabardine and in came a distinctive red, green and blue tartan. At the same time the school logo was altered so that the uniform badge now displays two young girls walking across a bridge, preparing for life, just as they will be doing at this school.

Top left: *HM Queen Elizabeth meets children from Newbridge Preparatory School on her visit to Wolverhampton in 1994.* ***Above left:*** *Former Headmistresses Olive Harvey (left) and Hedi Joss (right) join the present Headmistress, Marilyn Coulter to launch the building for the Future Appeal.* ***Right:*** *Pupils model their new school uniform.*

Care in the community

When someone is in need of care and treatment for cancer or other life threatening illness, it is not just the physical pain that requires addressing. There is also mental anguish that may be felt which also extends to the anxieties being experienced by friends and loved ones. Within our society there needs to be a framework that can offer services that alleviate both the physical and mental traumas that may touch people at a time when they are at their most vulnerable, and when they are least able to cope.

The Hospice movement came into being to provide a warm, secure and supportive environment at just such times of stress. It provides a chance for patients to live as full and as comfortable a life as possible, for however long that life may be. At the same time it respects the dignity of the patient, and provides peace of mind for relatives and carers. There also has to be a sense of realism whilst enabling both patients and families to come to terms with the rigours occasioned by serious illness.

Right: *Cedars Study Centre.*
Below: *Compton Hospice, 'The Hall'.*

Twenty years ago the need to provide such an establishment in Wolverhampton was identified. Financial support came from a number of sources, including the National Society for Cancer Relief, Institutions, Trusts, Groups and private individuals. Compton Hall, with a history going back to early Victorian times, was purchased and renovated, with the Duchess of Kent officially opening the Hospice on November 9th 1982.

Compton Hospice now serves a catchment area 1.2 million people, drawing from the population of Sandwell, Dudley, Walsall, Wolverhampton, South Staffs and East Shropshire. It provides specialist advice on symptom control and pain relief.

Situated in the suburbs of Wolverhampton the Hospice provides a 22 bed In-Patient unit, two Day Care Centres, Counselling, Physiotherapy, Home Care and Hospice at Home Services, a Chaplaincy Team and Out-Patient Department.

Currently over 500 patients and relatives receive care and support from Compton's services at any one time, 365 days of the year, completely free of charge.

In the second half of 2001 the Hospice purchased a new site - the Cedars, close to the main Hospice. These premises house the Fundraising and Trading Offices, whilst providing enlarged facilities for the busy Study Centre. Compton's expertise is now shared widely through the courses that are offered in Palliative Care, up to and including degree level with the support of Wolverhampton University.

The Lodge at the Cedars has also been converted into a purpose built Lymphoedema Clinic and Out-Patients Department. Not only do the specialist lymphoedema staff work on site, but also at New Cross Hospital, as do two further Clinical Nurse Specialists in partnership with the Wolverhampton Hospital Trust.

In April 2001 the new Hospice at Home Service was launched with some financial support from the New Opportunities Fund. This service enables some patients to remain in their own homes, and community, for those last few vital days of life, and has also been enlarged to allow for some respite care.

The growth of services also sees the need for a growth in income. In the current financial year over £4 million is needed to provide all the services to patients. Though supported by the six Health Authorities they serve, Compton Hospice still needs to raise over £2.8 million from voluntary income. This huge amount comes from individuals, support groups, companies, legacies and regular giving, as well as the 11 Charity Shops, and the Hospice's Weekly Lottery. Over 80 pence in every £1 is spent direct on patient care and the Hospice continues to be enormously grateful for the support shown by the communities they serve. This support is vital to the future of Compton Hospice as part of the community, just as the Hospice is important in the caring and professional role it plays within that community. It is a joint exercise, each needing the other.

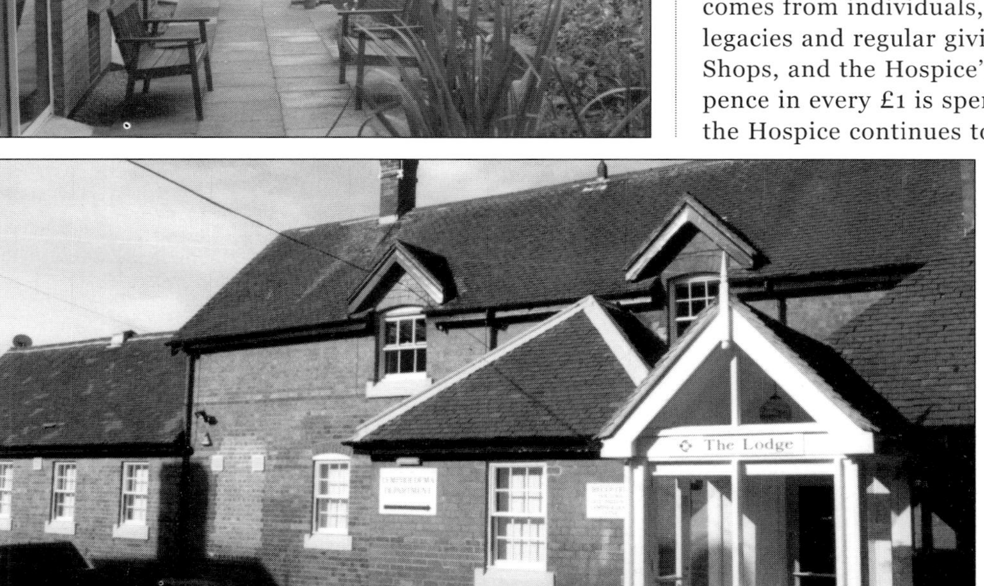

Top right: *Fundraising at the Cedars Family Fun Day, 2001.*
Above left: *A rear view of the Compton Hospice Ward.*
Left: *The Lymphoedema Clinic/ Outpatient Department.*

An electrifying performance for over 70 years

Burns and Dudgon Ltd is one of the Midlands' top electrical contractors, with experience in its field going back to before the war. These days it has two companies trading under its banner in Wolverhampton and Stourbridge.

The company has built up to such an extent that it employs about 40 staff and generates an annual turnover of £2 million. It is a member of the major electrical trade associations and is a company with a firm commitment to the future, as instanced by its involvement in and strong associations with apprenticeship schemes. These help to guarantee that new employees are given a thorough grounding in their trade as youngsters who can then make their way onto the fully trained workforce that provides such an excellent service to its customers.

The way in which Burns and Dudgon provides opportunities for staff development is obviously appreciated as there are many loyal and long serving employees, including some who are second and third generation family members. A secure and contented workforce is always more likely to deliver a more efficient and reliable service than one that is disgruntled and this has evidently been long acknowledged at Burns and Dudgon.

The company's founder members set up in business together c1930 and the limited company was formed in 1934. At first it traded out of a large house in Newhampton Road, but soon moved to first floor offices above a wedding and bridal services shop at the corner of St John Street and Dudley Street. Some of the first contracts included work on recharging accumulators for radios, but, even in the difficult economic climate of the inter war years, business boomed to such an extent that the firm soon expanded into premises at the old Mander Paints' canteen, at the bottom of St John Street.

A large retail outlet was established by the steps of the Central Arcade, selling Hoover products and all manner and types of light fittings. By now a modest contracting business had also developed quite nicely,

***Right:** Chris Walton waiting to set off in one of the firm's fleet of service vehicles.*
***Below:** A view of the retail premises in Newhampton Road West.*

though it needed an injection of further vigour to help it grow further.

When the town centre was redeveloped the company had to find new premises once again, this time on Harrow Street. At the end of the 1960s the remaining founder member, Ernie Dudgon, had sold out to a group of directors keen on expanding the business. Work was wide ranging, from house rewiring to commercial and industrial contracts.

There was a considerable amount of work carried out for the Ministry of Public Buildings and Works in the Midlands area. Other important contracts were won, including one with the notable architect Bertram Butler, Tettenhall Road. Further growth over the years led to more and more prestigious contracts being won as the firm's reputation for quality and reliability spread across the Black Country. Of particular note was electrical work for the Tarmac Building at Ettingshall, the Masonic Hall on Tettenhall Road, various public houses and a number of the branches of Lloyd's Bank. There were also refurbishments and upgrades for labour exchanges, DHSS offices and many other government departments too numerous to mention.

Burns and Dudgon made its next move to 48 Newhampton Road West in 1979 to allow for further expansion, bringing with it the old wooden office accommodation from Harrow Street that was re-erected at the rear as a store.

In more recent times major work has been carried out for such important clients as the Birmingham Hippodrome, refurbished for the introduction of the Royal Ballet, the National Sports Centre, Lilleshall, where two sports halls were completely refitted, and night clubs ranging from Brighton to Birmingham and from London to Manchester.

Towards the end of the 1990s saw a further change in the management and organisation of the company. Roger Beddows joined the company over 40 years ago, rising to become its managing director. He, Yvonne Beddows and Nigel Taylor conducted a management buy out of the company and are already reshaping it in order to meet the challenges that lie ahead as this century unfolds.

Top left: *A project completed in 2001, an 84 bedroom nursing home in Johnson Street, Wolverhampton.*
Left: *Electrician Gary Shilbrook putting the finishing touches to an installation.* ***Below:*** *Director Nigel Taylor estimating another project.*

Food for thought since 1945

As the 21st century unfolds Freshway Foods goes from strength to strength, as one of the country's major supplier of sandwiches, fillings, salads and seafood.

Having moved to Wolverhampton in 1959, from humble beginnings in Southport, Freshway has positively risen to the challenges of recent years in response to market forces and public demands. Whilst not losing sight of the traditional values, inherent within the business, the products and nature of production has dramatically changed.

What has not changed is the attitude of Graham and Alan Wright, the brothers whose hands are on the helm today, towards providing quality products at competitive prices in an atmosphere of teamwork that embraces management, staff, customers and suppliers. This philosophy, backed by a long standing reputation for quality and innovation, has helped the company establish itself as a leader within its field.

***Above:** Frank Wright, company founder, on the company's first delivery vehicle!*
***Below:** One of the firm's delivery vehicles in the 1960s.*

Today the Wright brothers, like their namesakes, are flying high and very much involved in running the business on a day to day basis.

But, how different it all was when their father, Frank Wright, founded the business in 1945. He flew around Southport on a trusty motorbike laying the foundations of what is today a multi-million pound business. From those humble beginnings, Frank, his wife Norma and nephew Maurice worked hard to create the core business of supplying quality seafood to the local community. Based on 20 years of experience within the fish trade they developed a range of quality seafood, sold pre-packed in pubs and clubs in the area.

The immediate post-war years were far from an easy time in which to set up a new venture. Money was tight but Frank worked hard, quickly establishing his place in this market. He was soon supplying selling agents covering parts of Merseyside and Lancashire, with occasional forays into the Wirral. With their baskets of cockles, prawns, mussels, shrimps and jellied eels they soon became a regular sight in the lounges and bars of local pubs, sports clubs, working men's clubs and branches of the British Legion. A bottle of vinegar was carried in the salesman's coat pocket and produced

Above: *A publicity shot of some of the products produced by Freshway in the 1980s.* ***Left:*** *An early advertisement for Wright's Shellfish.* ***Below:*** *The firm's logo used during the 1970s and 80s.*

For Fresh Shell Fish and Sea Food Delicacies

consult

WRIGHT'S SHELLFISH (SOUTHPORT) LTD

WOLVERHAMPTON AIRPORT

Tel.: FORDHOUSES 3666-7

Our Salesmen call on hundreds of clubs in the Midlands and serve thousands of satisfied club members and other patrons with Fresh Shell Fish in Hygienic Waxed Paper Bags.

CAN YOUR CLUB BE ANOTHER?

A Telephone call will bring immediate attention.

We are noted for our fresh Cockles, Mussels, Whelks, Oysters, Prawns, Buttered Shrimps, Fresh Crab, Scampi and the

FINEST JELLIED EELS IN THE MIDLANDS

Visit our unique new Shell Bar

at Perry Barr, Birmingham (adjacent Greyhound Stadium)

Open every day and evening (except Mondays) until Midnight for

Shell Fish Meals, Chips, and Snacks

with a flourish to add further piquancy to the little tub purchased.

As business prospered and the sales agents graduated from bicycles and motorbikes to cars and vans, Frank decided to expand what was then called Wright's Shellfish (Southport) Ltd to the West Midlands. His home base meant that in reaching larger conurbation's, such as Liverpool, Manchester and beyond, involved considerable travel, so he was determined to seek out a new base that gave easy access to a large centre of population. The range had now expanded to include the more exotic namely: oysters, scampi and crab amongst the usual cockles, mussels and prawns.

In 1959, he moved his whole enterprise to premises at Wolverhampton Airport. He established a fully equipped factory that was admirably situated at the centre of his new distribution area. In a short while his name and products became as well known in the Wolverhampton area as they had been on the Fylde coast.

By the end of the 1960s Wright's had also established a Seafood Restaurant at Perry Barr, near the greyhound stadium, as well as a number of other wholesale outlets. No Saturday night at the pub was complete without a tanner bag of cockles, liberally flavoured with Sarson's and washed down by a pint of Ansell's best.

1976 saw the move to Stafford Court, Wolverhampton, Freshway's home today. This was not the end of the story by a long way.

Having secured a prime position next to the heart of Britain's motorway system the company was to experience substantial

Above and below right: *Some of the range of sandwiches that the firm is currently producing.*
Right: *Freshway Foods' mobile retail unit in the Merry Hill Shopping Centre.*

change over the coming years. With changing market trends and customer tastes Freshway made a momentous decision to enter the sandwich and sandwich fillings market – this sparked the beginning of the future. The dramatic increase in product range lead to a name change to Freshway Seafood's, which was later to become Freshway Foods, this also occasioned a change from the long established fish logo as it no longer reflected the broader activity.

The company has not, however, lost sight of the core values of its traditional seafood heritage. The confidence and foresight of brothers Alan and Graham backed by enthusiastic and supportive wives resulted in major investments in the 1990s.

In addition to the existing seafood business, sandwiches and sandwich fillings became an integral part of the business. In 1995, with a request from one of Europe's leading brands to supply quality ready made sandwiches, that the current expansion and success story began. By the end of the 1990s Freshway expansion was snowballing to such an extent that the

company invested over £2.5 million in a new factory to meet projected production demands.

The prestigious new building was officially opened in 1999 with Coronation Street's Hayley (Julie Hesmondhalgh), Roy (David Neilson) and local MP Ken Purchase in attendance. This more than doubled the previous amount of production space available to a 32,000 square feet. Investment in the company did not end there, a further £1 million

Left: *The company's Stafford Road headquarters pictured in the 1980s.*

was invested in terms of new production equipment and warehousing facilities.

The family run business made sure that all the improvements were not concentrated upon its production facilities as it recognised the importance of a pleasant environment for its workforce. Money was also earmarked to upgrade staff facilities in terms of changing areas, showers and a new dining area - all of which are second to none!

What had been a staff of a mere 42 in the early 1990s has grown dramatically and now exceeds 250, with the most significant rise occurring in the last few years - turnover has increased by 100 per cent in the last three years

FRESHWAY® FOODS
Est. 1945

In 2000 Freshway was a finalist in the prestigious Birmingham Business Post Award, thus recognising it as a progressive company. A whole host of innovative products have been launched in the last few years, including such mouth watering sophisticated products as the Prawn and Salmon starter and Snow Crab mousse. New lines have also been added to Freshway's portfolio of products including layered salads and pasta salads, ensuring that Freshway Foods continue to move forward and take the lead in this dynamic market place. Freshway's dedication to supplying customers with quality products is reflected in the rigorous quality procedures which has led to the award of the nationally recognised British Retail Consortium Higher Accreditation.

The acquisition of Fredericks, the Telford based sandwich makers, has enabled the company to further expand the supply of sandwiches under the Freshway brand.

Further extensions at Stafford Court, completed in November 2001, proved that the only way forward for Freshway Foods is to build on the success of the past by keeping a 'seafaring' eye on market trends and consumer demands in the future!

Top centre: *Freshway's new identity for the new century.*
Above left: *Ken Purchase, MP, with company directors Graham Wright, Alan Wright and Maurice Wright, unveiling the flag celebrating Freshway's 55th Anniversary.*
Left: *Freshway Foods premises pictured in 2001.*

Children taking part in the celebrations for the Queen's coronation, 1953.

Acknowledgments

Birmingham Post & Mail
Alex Chatwin
Mrs M Eisenhofer
Janice Endean
Eardley Lewis
Brian Perry
Malcolm Cooper
Wolverhampton Photographic Society
Wolverhampton Archives & Local Studies
Wolverhampton Express & Star

Thanks are also due to
John Thornton who penned the editorial text
and Steve Ainsworth for his copywriting skills